f

d

50 Powerful Catalysts

INSTANT

for Group Interaction and

ICEBREAKERS

High-Impact Learning

SANDY CHRISTIAN, MSW
NANCY LOVING TUBESING, EdD

Printed in the United States of America
10 9 8 7 6 5 4

Library of Congress Cataloging-in-Publication Data
    Instant Icebreakers / Sandy Stewart Christian, Nancy Loving
Tubesing, editors.
    192 p.   23 cm.
    Includes bibliographical references.
    ISBN 1-57025-125-8
    1. Group relations training—Problems, exercises, etc.
  2. Interpersonal communication—Problems, exercises, etc.
  3. Group games. I. Christian, Sandy Stewart, Nancy Loving Tubesing.
  HM134.I68 1997
  302'.14—dc21   96-51244
                                                      CIP

Whole Person Associates Inc.
210 West Michigan
Duluth, MN 55802
(800) 247-6789

Acknowledgments

We are grateful to the many inspired and inspiring group leaders from whom we have learned over the past three decades. To youth group leaders, social workers, counselor educators, communications experts, systems theorists, teachers, family therapists, alcohol and drug abuse counselors, CPE supervisors, psychologists, corporate trainers, chaplains, OD consultants, group therapists, adult education specialists, professional colleagues, consciousness-raising groups, and especially to the thousands of individuals we've been privileged to work with in groups, classes, and workshops over the years—thanks for all you've taught us.

Special thanks to Carl Rogers, Virginia Satir, Fritz Perls, the NTL network, Lyman Coleman, Howard Gardner, David Lazear, AAMFT colleagues, Rene and Merle Fossum, Marilyn Mason, Murray Bowen, Peggy Papp, and Carl Whitaker, whose visionary concepts gave us the theory and shaped our understanding of human nature, learning, and group process.

Our deepest appreciation, as well, for those colleagues and mentors who gave us the opportunity to learn along with them: Dan Bergeland, Betty Bosdell, Hal Brown, Max Bruck, Chuck Dull, Jerry Epp, Rosemary Ferguson, Ed Fritze, Joel Goodman, Mary Graff, Lynn Jacobs, Norm Kagan, Mary Martin, Bill and Stephanie Miller, Lyn Clark Pegg, Len and Lori Rand, Anne Wilson Schaef, Gloria Singer, Mary O'Brien Sippel, Mary Ann Stehr, Sally Strosahl, and especially Don Tubesing, whose insight and creativity has been a constant source of inspiration.

Susan Gustafson, editorial director at Whole Person Associates, truly deserves our utmost appreciation for her organizational clarity, deft editing hand, and patience with us as authors. As always, she has strengthened our work substantially and added those special touches that make this volume more helpful and user friendly. Heather

Isernhagen cheerfully (and magically!) transformed our handwritten drafts into actual printed pages and made the worksheets come alive with her computer graphics savvy. Our thanks also to Kathy DeArmond-Lundblad for her page crafting and meticulous proofreading , and to Jeff Brownell for the smashing cover. You all have been a joy to work with.

Sandy Stewart Christian, MSW
Nancy Loving Tubesing, EdD

January 1977

P81934

Table of Contents

© 1997 Whole Person Associates 210 W Michigan Duluth MN 55802-1908   800-247-6789

Self-Awareness

Change Agents

Resources

© 1997 Whole Person Associates 210 W Michigan Duluth MN 55802-1908   800-247-6789

Introduction

We live on the spectacular shores of Lake Superior, where icebreakers are a common sight on the winter lakescape, clearing the way for vessels headed into or out of the harbor or freeing ships stuck in the massive deep pack ice.

What does a Lake Superior icebreaker do? The same thing a good group icebreaker does: It opens the way. It sets the course. It clears a path. It facilitates movement. It cuts through barriers. It breaks up resistance.

We believe that icebreakers are much more than fun and games. *Instant Icebreakers* is filled with brief group activities that help people connect with each other and warm up to a task or topic. These creative, interactive processes open the way to learning. They set the course and clear a path for the important information that follows. They cut through barriers and invite participants to get involved in their own learning process. We hope you will agree.

All of our teaching designs and group activities are grounded in some basic principles about adult learning that are often overlooked in the actual process of adult education in seminars, workshops, and training events.

Assumptions about learning

People learn better when they are actively involved–physically, mentally, interpersonally, and emotionally. People also learn better when they apply a concept, principle, or skill to their own life. Creative group activities foster this kind of active, practical learning. Adult learners learn best in an environment that honors their life experience. Icebreakers offer opportunities for adult learners to pool their shared wisdom and learn from each other.

People learn differently. Some learn best by hearing, some by seeing,

© 1997 Whole Person Associates 210 W Michigan Duluth MN 55802-1908   800-247-6789

some by reflecting, some by interacting, some by doing, some by talking, some by incorporating music or rhythm, some by solving problems. The best teaching incorporates elements of all learning styles to assure that everyone is hooked into the learning process.

Icebreakers offer an opportunity to appeal to a variety of learning styles, helping people with diverse learning styles to get on board with a topic or issue.

People learn better in a safe environment, when their defenses are down. Icebreakers help to lower these defenses. Everyone is afraid of, or at least concerned about, what others think of them. Telling personal stories is a powerful connecting tool for people. If everyone speaks within the first five to ten minutes, people's anxiety level diminishes and they are more ready to learn. Icebreakers provide an opportunity for everyone to get involved on equal footing as they make quick connections with others in the group.

People learn better in a supportive group context. Icebreakers can establish instant rapport. No matter how different individuals are, any two people can find a point of connection and identification, a place where their needs, experiences, or agendas overlap. One of the purposes of an icebreaker is to help people find this commonality, this connecting point.

Given this philosophical framework, we have collected a variety of engaging processes that have been used successfully in many settings by trainers, group leaders, and educators from many professional backgrounds. We offer them here with a few guidelines for effective use.

How to use this book

We have tried to make the format of *Instant Icebreakers* easy to use for both preparation and presentation. Each icebreaker includes a brief description, explicit learning goals, approximate timing, an indication of appropriate group size and setting, and a list of materials needed.

The process is outlined step by step, using special symbols to help you lead the process effectively.

● Indicates a chalktalk point that introduces a key concept, offers tips to the participants, or summarizes learnings. Expand or adapt to meet your needs.

➤ Indicates an instruction to be read out loud to participants. Take special care that you understand what happens at each step and estimate your timing.

☞ *The hand symbol is a caution sign to the leader. Pay close attention to these warnings about presession preparation, cautions about possible pitfalls, suggestions for facilitating group process, examples to use in illustrating a point, and comments on timing.*

Most icebreakers include a Variations section with recommendations and adaptations for different settings and time frames. Companion scripts, handouts, and worksheets are at the end of the exercise.

Nearly all the icebreakers in this book are written with the workshop or large audience setting in mind. Each activity includes instructions for creating smaller discussion groups and approximate times for each step of the activity. Keep in mind that the size of the group determines the actual timing. With more people, every step takes more time.

When to use icebreakers

Don't limit yourself to a single get-acquainted process at the beginning of a session. Be creative! Try an icebreaker after a coffee break to get the group refocused. Try one as a tool for shifting gears or making transitions to a new content area. Try an icebreaker at the end of a session. Many of the processes work well to provide closure, affirmation, or reinforcement of learning. Try an icebreaker whenever the group energy flags. Just make sure that whatever activity you choose truly reinforces your learning objectives and goals.

© 1997 Whole Person Associates 210 W Michigan Duluth MN 55802-1908   800-247-6789

How to choose icebreakers

Choose icebreakers to fit your topic. Don't just play games. As you search for creative activities, keep your learning objectives in mind. Make sure the activity you choose moves the group and individuals in the desired direction. Feel free to adapt any process to fit your content and goals.

Choose icebreakers to fit your setting. When possible, rearrange your setting so you have ample room for group activity and flexible seating for small groups. Although it's almost impossible to form trios, quartets, and small groups in auditorium-style seating, adapt small group activities by pairing up neighbors, or have alternate rows turn around for discussion with neighbors in front or behind.

Choose icebreakers to fit your audience. Kindergarten teachers respond differently from CEOs. Engineers and artists have different tolerance for ambiguity. College students and golden agers may have different comfort levels. Working with groups of people who know each other well is quite different from working with groups of strangers. Know your audience and select appropriate activities. But also take some risks. Icebreakers give people an excuse to stretch their normal comfort zone a bit—usually with very positive outcomes.

Choose icebreakers to fit your tolerance for ambiguity, disruption, and resistance. Icebreakers may challenge your need to be in control. In every group there will be some folks who won't like a particular activity. It may take some cajoling and group pressure to get them to participate in an icebreaker. Some people may have a disappointing or even negative experience. But the majority are likely to have a very positive experience and learn a great deal. Some people may even prefer the group interaction and creative activities to your more one-dimensional presentations.

Choose icebreakers to fit your skill level and savvy about group dynamics. As you consider the creative options in this book and the wealth of other resources available, pay attention to your own reactions. If a process seems too complicated or off the wall for you, try something simpler or more conventional. Some processes that are dynamite with a big audience fall flat in a small group. Experiment until you find a repertoire of techniques that fit you and your typical audiences. But don't be lulled into complacency. Stretch your comfort zone by experimenting with at least one new technique in every group.

Ground rules for giving instructions

Giving instructions to a group takes real skill and lots of practice. Inexperienced leaders usually make the mistake of giving too many, too complicated instructions, too quickly.

First, get people's attention. Whenever you encourage active participation you need effective strategies to stay in charge. We usually use a harmonica or wooden train whistle to interrupt small group discussions. But a bugle or a drum roll would be just as effective and entertaining.

Never try to talk when there is noise in the room. This is especially important when you are doing active icebreakers. Blow your whistle to get people settled down or try whispering instead of shouting. We prefer to use a microphone whenever the group is larger than twenty—it saves your voice and allows a much wider range of volume.

With a brief icebreaker, give step-by-step instructions first. Then demonstrate, if possible. Don't give too many instructions at once. In this book, we have tried to help you pace yourself by breaking the instructions into separate, numbered steps.

In a longer, more complicated exercise, give the big picture first, then guide the process in segments, explaining as you go along. Be sure to allow plenty of time for participants to do the activity before giving the next set of instructions.

Always give instructions for forming small groups first. Then wait until the groups are settled to assign their task and give detailed instructions.

Be prepared. Always work through an exercise first yourself so you can anticipate questions. Brainstorm examples appropriate for your audience. Choose some personal experiences to use as illustrations.

The rest is up to you. Enjoy!

© 1997 Whole Person Associates 210 W Michigan Duluth MN 55802-1908   800-247-6789

Introductions

This section includes sixteen simple but effective processes for initial meetings and greetings that set a positive tone for group learning.

1 Tear a Tag

Participants create unique, personalized name tags by tearing out shapes symbolic of themselves.

Goals

To get acquainted with other participants.

To stimulate self-disclosure.

Group size

Unlimited.

Time

5–10 minutes.

Materials

Construction paper; string cut into 30" lengths (one for each participant); markers; paper punch.

Process

1. Give everyone a sheet of construction paper, a piece of string, and a marker, and instruct participants to create their own personalized name tag. (2–3 minutes)

   ➤ Tear your paper into a shape such as a heart, a butterfly, or a football, that is symbolic of you.

   ➤ Write your name on your tag, then punch holes at each corner of the top of your shape, pull the string through the holes, and tie the ends together to create a hanger for your name tag.

   ➤ Put your name tag on for introductions.

2. Instruct participants to sit in a circle and introduce themselves briefly using their name tag creations as a means of sharing on a personal level. (5 minutes)

☞ *For groups larger than 10–12 people, consider one of the alternatives suggested in the variations below.*

➤ Introduce yourself by giving your name and explaining your name tag to the group.

　➤ Tell why you chose the particular shape you did, and what it says about you as a person.

　➤ Take about 1 minute each.

3. Reconvene the group and introduce the first topic on your agenda.

Variations

▪ With groups of 12 or more, divide into several smaller groups for sharing in Step 2. Use color of name tag or another strategy that fits your setting and audience.

▪ With groups of 30 or more, invite participants to mill around, introduce themselves to three different people, and share name tag stories with each other.

▪ For groups that will be together for an entire day, consider a two-part icebreaker. Before your first break, collect all name tags and put them in a box or basket. At some later point when the group needs energizing, invite everyone to pull out a tag and find the person who matches it. When all are wearing their original name tags again, move on to the next agenda item.

For extra fun, divide large groups into two teams and have a race to see which team can match all their tags with the rightful owners first. Whenever people are matched with their tags, they are captured, and join the team who discovered them.

2 Meet Me on Madison Avenue

Advertising images and slogans bring participants together in this novel introductory process that explores media impact on self-care habits.

Goals

To meet other participants.

To explore implicit promises and actual realities of advertising for health-related products.

Group size

Unlimited. Works best with large groups.

Time

10–20 minutes.

Materials

Pairs of name tags with a logo or image of a health-related product mounted on one tag and an advertising slogan for that product mounted on the second tag; extra blank name tag for each person.

Process

☞*Prior to your workshop or presentation, collect a variety of magazine ads for products that make health claims, such as over-the-counter drugs or products that affect health, such as soft drinks and snack foods. Make sure you have a slogan and a picture or logo for each product. Create a name tag for each participant gluing on either a logo/image or a slogan (e.g., a picture of the Coke logo on one tag and the words "It's the real thing" on the next).*

1. Hand out name tags randomly as people arrive, making sure that everyone gets a tag and puts it on as they enter the room.

2. When you are ready to begin the icebreaker, announce that participants will meet another participant on Madison Avenue, as they explore advertisements for health-related products. Give instructions for finding partners and discussing the implicit promises and actual realities of health-related products. (3–4 minutes)

> On your name tag is either an image of a health-related product or an advertising slogan for a product. Every product has a matching slogan. Every slogan has a matching product.

> Look at your product or read your slogan, then stand up and walk around until you find the person wearing the matching product image or slogan.

> When you find your partner, introduce yourself and spend 2–3 minutes discussing the image and slogan.

>> First, what's the promise held out by the product and slogan? What does Madison Avenue tell you to expect?

>> Second, what's the reality of this health product? What do you really get with this product?

☞ *As people are talking, circulate and distribute a fresh blank name tag to each person.*

3. After 3–4 minutes, interrupt and invite participants to create more realistic descriptions.

> Take 2–3 minutes to decide on a more realistic description of your product—a new slogan that tells it like it really is. You might describe Coke as "a carbonated, caffeinated drink that tastes good to some but has the power to rust nails."

> Whatever realistic description you compose, write it on your new name tag and stick the new slogan/tag below or alongside your original name tag.

4. Ask each pair to introduce themselves to the large group and share their original product and slogan and their new slogan.

☞ *This should be a quick go-around, without discussion or debate about health images and slogans. Keep it moving and strive for a lighthearted, humorous atmosphere. In large groups, just ask for a few examples.*

5. Ask each pair to join two other pairs, forming groups of six people. When groups are settled, give instructions for further discussion about the effects of advertising on self-care. (5 minutes)

   ➤ Discuss the positive and negative ways advertising affects your self-care.

   ➤ You have 5 minutes for discussion. Make sure everyone gets a chance to contribute.

6. Reconvene the large group and solicit observations about the effects of advertising on self-care.

7. Summarize group responses, building bridges to your next learning component.

Variations

▧ For women's groups, select products that are directed toward female consumers (e.g., bras, beauty products, perfume, feminine hygiene products, vitamins with iron, estrogen, exercise videos). For men's groups, select products and ads that are geared for the male market (e.g., alcohol, deodorants, dandruff shampoo).

▧ For couples and families, focus on ads implying that happy, healthy relationships or homes will result from use of products such as laundry soap, storm windows, toilet cleaner, or canned soup.

▧ For recovery or prevention groups, choose ads that glorify the use of alcohol, romanticize drinking, or minimize its effects. In group discussions, focus on the hooks Madison Avenue uses to lure people of different ages and backgrounds.

3 Line Dance

Participants introduce themselves while performing a simple line dance that anyone can do.

Goals

To make contact with other participants and learn everyone's name.

To create a relaxed, casual atmosphere for the group.

Group size

Unlimited, as long as the room is large enough for group members to form a line and for leaders to move down the line with unrestricted movement.

Time

5–10 minutes.

Materials

None.

Process

☞ *Practice this routine before springing it on a group. The instructions can be confusing.*

1. Ask everyone to stand and, if necessary, move chairs and other obstacles so that there is a large open space available for this introductory country dance. Explain to participants that they will be introducing themselves to other group members by using a simple line dance.

2. Once everyone is in place, explain the steps of the Contact Virginia Reel, demonstrating each move as you go.

☞ *Pair up with the "odd" person or borrow a partner to walk through the process as you describe it.*

➤ Grab your neighbor as a partner and line up with other pairs in the middle of the open space.

> Turn and stand facing your partner, shoulder to shoulder with the other couples so that the whole group forms two parallel lines.

> Now stretch out the line so each couple has a bit of elbow room.

➤ During this dance you will be introducing yourself to everyone in the line opposite you.

➤ The first two people in the line become the leaders and start the dance.

> **Leaders**, look at your partner; introduce yourselves by first name.

> Then step toward each other, interlock right arms at the elbow, and swing around.

➤ Each of the leaders then move down the line to the person who was standing in line next to your partner.

> Introduce yourself by first name to this person, who in turns responds by saying their own name. Then interlock arms and take a swing.

> **Leaders**, continue to move all the way down the line, introducing yourselves and spinning around with each new person, until you reach the end of the line. When you reach the end of the line, take your places across from each other at the end of the line.

> Everyone else in the line, maintain your position and listen to the introductions as the leaders swing down the line.

➤ When one couple finishes the reel, the two people left at the front of the line become the new leaders and begin another get acquainted dance.

© 1997 Whole Person Associates 210 W Michigan Duluth MN 55802-1908   800-247-6789

> **New leaders**, introduce yourself to your partner, do your swing, then move down the line introducing yourself to people as you swing along.

> Repeat the dance over and over, until everyone has been a leader.

☞ *If space is tight, encourage people to move up in line after they've swung with the leader.*

Variations

▨ To liven things up, add music and ask participants to perform the movements more quickly in time with the music. This could be done as a second round of introductions or as an energizer after a few hours of sitting.

4 Magnetic Personality

In this esteem-building exercise, participants identify facets of
their personality that draw people to them.

Goals

To identify and affirm positive personality traits.
To get acquainted with other participants.

Group size

Unlimited.

Time

5–10 minutes.

Materials

Magnetic Personality worksheets.

Process

1. Start with a statement expressing the idea that everyone in the
   room has something about them or their personality that
   draws other people to them. Announce that you will be asking
   everyone to explore their own magnetic personality.

2. Hand out **Magnetic Personality** worksheets and ask participants to affirm their unique, appealing qualities or traits. (2–3
   minutes)

   ➤ Think about the unique, likable, interesting, engaging qualities you have that draw people toward you like a magnet.

      ➤ Perhaps you have a winning smile, an interesting face,
      a lively mind, a rich life experience, a sense of humor,
      a warm, friendly attitude, an engaging laugh, an ac-
      cepting manner, a calming style, a soothing voice, or a
      positive spirit.

© 1997 Whole Person Associates 210 W Michigan Duluth MN 55802-1908   800-247-6789

➤ Write your positive, attractive qualities on your magnet.
  ➤ Don't be shy or modest. This is a time to claim your best
    traits or personal gifts.

3. Instruct participants to use their magnetic personalities to
   meet other participants. (2–3 minutes)
   ➤ Stand up, mill around, and pair up with someone whom
     you would like to know better.
   ➤ Start by sharing what drew you to this particular person,
     then share your own magnetic personality traits with your
     partner.
   ➤ Take turns talking about what you think draws other people
     to you.

4. After 2–3 minutes, instruct participants to move around,
   find a new partner, and repeat the process of sharing magnetic personalities.
   ☞ *Repeat the process until time or the energy of the group runs out.*

Variations

▨ With groups of 6–10 participants, instead of using the worksheet, have participants sit in a circle facing each other. Pass
   around a large magnet, asking people to hold it as they introduce themselves and tell the group about their own magnetic
   personality traits.

▨ As an affirming group prize, give everyone small toy magnets
   to keep as symbols of their ability to draw others to them.

MAGNETIC PERSONALITY

My magnetic personality traits:

5 Fine Fettle Shakes

In this uproarious exercise, participants create unique hand-shakes for greeting other group members with good humor at the beginning, middle, and end of the session.

Goals

To build cohesion and a positive group culture.

To promote fun and goodwill among participants.

Group size

Unlimited. Works best with larger groups.

Time

5–10 minutes.

Materials

None.

Process

1. Begin by declaring, "I'm in fine fettle today," as you demonstrate a variety of greetings such as traditional handshakes, high fives, and hugs.

   ☞ *Enlist a volunteer from the audience to help you with this quick demonstration.*

2. Tell participants that you think it would be fun for the group to have its very own unique greetings or handshakes, which could be used for different purposes during the learning experience: a get acquainted shake, an energizer shake, and an affirmative shake.

3. Designate three areas of the room, one for each shake and assign people to one of the groups, based on birthdays (January to April), (May to August), and (September to December).

4. As soon as groups are gathered, give instructions for creating fine fettle shakes.

   ➤ Group 1 is the *starter shake* group. Your job is to create a unique handshake designed for early greetings with other participants, that will convey good wishes for the upcoming day together.

   ➤ Group 2 is the *going strong* group. Your job is to invent a special handshake appropriate for mid-group activities, something that will be energizing and bolstering for participants whenever the group needs a boost.

   ➤ Group 3 is the *you did it* group. You are to develop an unusual handshake that affirms people for their learning or achievements during this session, and could be used to bid people farewell at the end of the meeting.

   ➤ Each group has 3 minutes to develop your shake and prepare to demonstrate it for the large group.

      ➤ Feel free to be outrageous, original, and funny while creating a shake that you think all participants would be comfortable doing.

5. When 3–5 minutes are up, ask each group to demonstrate their shake for the large group. Then instruct Group 1 to lead all participants in a *fine fettle starter shake*. (1 minute)

   ➤ Everyone walk around the room and introduce yourself to as many people as you can in 1 minute, using the *fine fettle starter shake* as demonstrated by Group 1.

6. Ask everyone to return to their seat, and explain that the *fine fettle going strong shake* and *fine fettle you did it shake* will be used later.

7. Later in the session, when people seem to need an energizing break, repeat Step 5 with Group 2 demonstrating the *going strong shake* mixer.

8. Close your session or workshop with a demonstration of the *you did it shake* from Group 3 and a series of farewell shakes.

Variations

Feel free to change the names of the shakes to suit your audience, developing *salesperson's salutations* for marketing teams, *worker's welcomes* for employee/staff groups; *helper's hails* for human service professionals; *banker's bows* for financial advisors and credit counselors; *police officer's pumps* for law enforcement officials; *teacher's tributes* for groups of educators, *clergy curtsies* for pastors and spiritual leaders, etc.

The inspiration for this icebreaker came from Bob Czimbal's welcoming workshop at the 1994 National Wellness Conference at Stevens Point, Wisconsin. His book, Stress Survival Kit, *is filled with energetic group activities like this one.*

6 Slow Disclosure

Participants slowly warm up to each other in this gentle get-to-know-you process.

Goals

To foster an atmosphere of trust.

To get acquainted and share personal information at a comfortable pace.

Group size

Unlimited, as long as there is space for small groups to meet with some degree of privacy.

Time

10–15 minutes.

Materials

List of get-acquainted questions developed by trainer in advance, and written in large print on flipchart or transparency (for overhead projector); newsprint sheet and marker for each participant; masking tape.

Process

Create a list of three to six questions appropriate to your audience and topic (see the list on page 20 for ideas). Be sure to begin with low-threat questions before moving to those that require more self-disclosure.

1. Introduce the icebreaker by stating the goals (to begin getting acquainted and feeling comfortable with other participants) and describing the process (people will be sharing whatever information they choose to in small groups).

© 1997 Whole Person Associates 210 W Michigan Duluth MN 55802-1908   800-247-6789

2. Give instructions for forming triads.

> Get together with two people you do not know well.

> Find a place where the three of you can sit down together and share privately.

>> *Use the time when people are forming groups to hang the newsprint list of get-acquainted questions in a place easily visible to all participants. Or use an overhead projector if this is easier.*

3. When everyone has joined a trio, give each group three sheets of newsprint and three markers as you explain the process of slow disclosure. (7–10 minutes)

> Write your first name across the top of your newsprint.

> Get acquainted with your partners one step at a time.

>> Write your response to the *first question only* on your newsprint.

>> When everyone is ready, go around the group, taking turns revealing your responses and explaining why you chose this particular response.

>> Share only as much as you care to.

> After everyone has shared responses to the first question, move on to the second question and repeat the process, moving down the list of questions, writing answers on your newsprint, and sharing responses with your partners.

> If you finish before other groups, feel free to make up your own questions and answer them.

4. After 8–10 minutes, reconvene the large group and acknowledge that participants now know at least two people in the group better than they did before. Encourage participants to build on this trust by gradually getting acquainted with one another during breaks or other opportunities for sharing during the workshop.

Variations

Tailor some questions to the interests or concerns of your audience. Prepare family-oriented questions for parenting or family life education groups, job-related questions for work groups, health-focused questions for wellness groups, gender-specific questions for men's or women's groups, etc.

GET-ACQUAINTED QUESTIONS

Begin icebreakers with brief, open-ended questions of a nonsensitive nature on relatively neutral topics that are unlikely to cause controversy or embarrassment and require low risk self-disclosure. Answers are usually brief.

What is your lucky number?
What is your favorite color?
What is one of your hobbies?
What is your favorite TV show?
What is your favorite place in your home town or city?
What is your favorite kind of car?
What is your favorite sports team?
What is your favorite soft drink?
What is your favorite boy's name? What is your favorite girl's name?
What country would you most like to visit?

Move on to questions requiring more self-disclosure about somewhat sensitive issues. Responses usually take a bit more thought and time.

What would be an ideal vacation for you?
What is one source of pride and joy in your life?
What are you hoping to learn in this experience?
What is difficult for you about change?
What is one stressful thing about your workplace?
What is one skill you could teach to others?
What is the one value you treasure most?
How would you describe your leadership style?
What are the qualities of a good friend? (supervisor/teacher/parent/employee/learner)
What three adjectives would your colleagues (subordinates/family/friends) use to describe you?

Be cautious with questions that require more self-disclosure on potentially sensitive or intimate issues. Don't ask questions like these unless you're planning to follow up in depth during the session or workshop or know your audience very well.

What life challenges are you facing right now?
In what ways are you like your mother? (father/boss/partner)
What is your biggest regret in life?
What is your biggest achievement in life?
If you had the power to change yourself, where would you start?
What contributions have you made to your community?
What crisis in your life have you weathered successfully?
What was one of your most embarrassing moments?

7 Library Cards

Conversation about favorite books is the focus of this stimulat-ing get-acquainted process.

Goals

To get acquainted.

To share influential books and other sources of mental stimulation.

Group size

Unlimited.

Time

5–10 minutes.

Materials

Library Card worksheets; masking tape.

Process

1. Pass out **Library Card** worksheets and invite participants to reflect on past and present sources of mental stimulation by identifying books that have been highly influential in their life and by listing other ways they exercise and stimulate their minds. (3–4 minutes)

   ➤ Write your name on the top of your library card.

   ➤ For each stage of your life, fill in the remaining blanks with titles of the most influential or memorable books you read during that period.

   ➤ At the bottom of your card, write two other significant sources of mental stimulation (e.g., puzzles, theater, politi-cal discussion, public radio or TV, dance, meditation, music) that you use to nourish your mind.

2. After 2–4 minutes, ask people to pair up with another participant and share important library card data. (6–7 minutes)
> Stand up and mill around the room, comparing library cards.
> When you find someone whose library card list of books is
intriguing to you, pair up with that person.
>> Take turns talking about the books on your library card,
telling why or how they were so influential in your life.
>> Tell your partner about other ways besides reading that
bring mental stimulation into your life.
>> Each person has 3 minutes to share.

3. When about 6 minutes have passed, interrupt participants
and ask them to post their library cards on a wall so that other
participants might satisfy their curiosity by reading through
the lists of books. Provide them with masking tape and, when
all library cards are hung, encourage people to explore the
group library.

Variations

■ This exercise could focus on other methods of learning, such
as visual, auditory, and kinesthetic. For visual, consider movies or TV shows; for auditory, music or conversations; for
kinesthetic, influential experiences with touch or movement.

■ This is an excellent exercise for parenting groups because
recalling powerful learning experiences encourages discussion
about stimulating children's minds.

■ In a therapy group, invite participants to recall significant
(good or bad) "touching" experiences for each time period.
This process can be especially powerful for people dealing
with abuse issues. Be prepared.

© 1997 Whole Person Associates 210 W Michigan Duluth MN 55802-1908   800-247-6789

LIBRARY CARD

Library Card: A49365   Expires _____

Name _____

The most influential (memorable) book I read

as a child _____

in high school _____

in college or as a young adult _____

as an adult _____

Two other significant sources of mental stimulation

   1.

   2.

8 Playground

This lighthearted exercise celebrates the importance of play throughout life.

Goals

To reinforce the importance of play for health and happiness.

To appreciate the variety of ways people play.

To use play stories as a way of getting acquainted.

Group size

Unlimited.

Time

10–15 minutes.

Materials

Playground worksheets.

Process

1. Distribute **Playground** worksheets and announce that, before getting down to work, participants will spend some time reflecting on the ways they play.

2. Guide participants through the reflection process, giving lots of playful examples for each life stage. (5 minutes)
   ➤ Take a few minutes to consider your patterns of play over your lifetime. For each stage of life, write as many examples as you can remember of playful activities you enjoyed.
   ➤ **As a child**, did you enjoy playing imaginary games with friends (pretend school or theater or cowboys and Indians), playing dress-up with adult clothes, swimming in a country lake or city pool, playing team sports like baseball or soccer, climbing trees and exploring the country woods?

© 1997 Whole Person Associates 210 W Michigan Duluth MN 55802-1908   800-247-6789

➤ Jot down several examples of playful activities you enjoyed as a child.

➤ **As an adolescent,** did you like hanging out with friends, listening to music, going to dances or high school sports events, having sleepovers with friends, riding horses or waterskiing, or going to movies?

➤ Record your adolescent play preferences.

➤ **As an adult, when you are alone,** do you enjoy dancing in your living room, going to plays, drawing or painting, hiking, photography, computer games, reading, cooking, walking on the beach, building furniture, working on car engines, restoring antiques, or watching old movies?

➤ Write down examples of your solitary play as an adult.

➤ **As an adult, when with friends,** do you like playing on a softball or volleyball team, acting in a local theater, throwing a party, snowmobiling, playing cards, celebrating birthdays, playing board games, having picnics, going bowling, traveling, or sharing meals?

➤ What forms of group playing do you indulge in as an adult?

➤ **As an adult, within your family,** do you enjoy telling family stories and jokes, wrestling or tickling, playing word games, watching movies together, baking cookies, gathering at the cabin, boating, swimming, building a family project together, or reading cartoon books and funny comics to each other?

➤ What are your favorite forms of family play?

3. Form small groups of 4–6 people. When groups are settled, give instructions for introductions. (5 minutes)

➤ Starting with the youngest member of your group, introduce yourself and share several favorite play experiences from childhood to adulthood.

➤ Continue sharing in order of age around the group, with each person taking about a minute.

4. After 4–5 minutes, interrupt the groups and invite them to recommend playful activities to use during the remainder of the session.

➤ Decide together which play idea you've discussed you would like to recommend that the whole group try as an energizer.

➤ Choose an activity that can be quickly and easily done by all participants, without risk of physical injury. (For example, skipping or hopping is probably okay, but cartwheels are not).

➤ Write your idea or recommendation on a slip of paper.

5. After 2 minutes, collect play ideas and recommendations from all groups and put them in a jar or hat. At key times during the session or workshop, select one at random to use as an energizer.

Variations

■ This exercise works well as a prelude to a workshop for couples or families. Play can be interjected as a fun way to build intimacy and trust.

Thanks to Michael Metz, PhD, Director of the University of Minnesota Program in Human Sexuality, for reminding us again about the importance of playfulness and creating the sequence of questions in the worksheet.

© 1997 Whole Person Associates 210 W Michigan Duluth MN 55802-1908   800-247-6789

PLAYGROUND

As a child, what I did to play

_____

_____

_____

As an adolescent, what I did to play

_____

_____

_____

As an adult, what I do to play

   Alone

_____

_____

_____

_____

   With friends

_____

_____

_____

_____

   With family

_____

_____

_____

_____

9 Hats

Participants make a pile of hats representing different roles they play and talk about feelings associated with wearing each hat.

Goals

To get to know other participants.

To explore social roles and feelings about playing these roles.

Group size

Unlimited.

Time

20 minutes.

Materials

Strips of plain heavyweight paper about 24" long and 3" wide (butcher paper or brown wrapping paper work well; computer paper will do in a pinch); watercolor markers; several bottles of glue or glue sticks (or tape or staplers); scissors.

Process

☞ *To save time, prepare the strips of paper in advance. You will need approximately eight strips per person. Bring extra paper and scissors along, in case you need more. Participants can cut their own extra strips if needed.*

1. Explain that participants will introduce themselves to each other by telling about some of the social roles they play—the hats they wear—and how they feel when playing these roles. Define *role* in a brief chalktalk.

    ● **A role is a socially expected behavior pattern** that is determined by a person's status in a particular society. Common

© 1997 Whole Person Associates 210 W Michigan Duluth MN 55802-1908   800-247-6789

roles include teacher, student, parent, child, friend, boss, employee, house cleaner, public servant, and citizen.

2. Divide participants into small groups of 6–8 people and give each group a stack of paper strips, glue, and markers. Then instruct participants to make a variety of hats symbolic of some of the roles they play at home, at work, and in the wider community. (5 minutes)

   ➤ Each person take several paper strips, a marker, and glue.
   ➤ Make a paper hat or headband for each role you play.
   > Use a different strip for each role (e.g., mother, disciplinarian, cook, nurse, chauffeur, business manager, volunteer, consumer, Sunday school teacher, Rotarian, concerned citizen).
   > Write the role in large letters on the strip.
   > Then form a ring with each strip and glue the ends together to make a circular hat that fits your head.
   > Make sure the role is showing on the outside.

   ☞ *Demonstrate how to make the hats by making one for yourself and labeling it **group leader**.*

   ➤ You should end up with a pile of paper hats symbolizing several roles—perhaps six or eight or even ten hats.

3. Instruct participants to introduce themselves to other members of their group by sharing their various roles and feelings associated with performing these roles. (8–10 minutes)

   ➤ The person with the most hats goes first.
   > Put one of your hats on your head, describe the role it represents, and briefly share how you typically feel when you are wearing this hat or fulfilling this role.
   > Put on the rest of your hats one-by-one, describing your roles and feelings for each.
   > Take 2 minutes to show off the many hats you wear.
   ➤ The person with the second most hats goes next. Take turns

going around the group, putting on each of your hats and describing feelings you have about each role.

4. When participants have finished sharing hats and feelings, ask everyone to return to their seats. Put on your group leader hat and playfully describe your feelings as you lead the group into the workshop.

Variations

■ If you are working with groups of families, ask people to stay with their family groups when they make hats and to focus on roles they play within their family.

■ Hats can be made for roles at work or on work teams. This is a good exercise for staff retreats when people may be exploring work roles and relationships in depth.

■ For more creativity and variety, use newspapers (comics are nice) to fold sailor hats, bonnets, or pressman's caps. Or substitute paper plates with ribbon ties.

10 Alphabet Free Association

Participants get to know each other—and themselves—from A to Z.

Goals

To explore life stress.

To share stories and possible happy endings with other group members.

Group size

Unlimited.

Time

15–20 minutes.

Materials

Alphabet Associations worksheet.

Process

1. Engage participants in a short, humorous free association game using words relevant to your audience or topic and asking people to shout out associations to each word. (1 minute)

2. Invite everyone to play another association game using the alphabet to discover personal stress and get acquainted. Distribute **Alphabet Associations** worksheets and guide participants through the process. (5–6 minutes)

   ➤ As quickly as you can, go through the alphabet list, jotting down the first word that comes to mind for each letter of the alphabet.

      ➤ Do not censor yourself or think too hard or long about your associations; just write the first word that comes to mind.

☞ *Pause here until most people are through the alphabet.*

➤ Look over your list of alphabet associations and circle the words that jump out at you. It's likely that these words are particularly relevant to you at this time of your life. They may hold the key to a difficult situation or shed light on your stress level or just reflect your current mood.

☞ *Wait until people have selected key words.*

➤ Now take 4 minutes and write a story or paragraph using the words you circled. Include a moral to your story. (4 minutes)

> Don't worry about grammar or other literary skills.

> Be playful and write whatever you want. There is no right way to write your story.

☞ *When 4 minutes are nearly up, remind participants to write a moral to their story.*

3. Ask participants to form groups of 5–6 people by finding others whose last name begins with the same letter as theirs.

☞ *Encourage groups to sit down as soon as they have five or six like-lettered members. Help the "leftovers" form alphabet soup groups of random letters.*

4. When all groups are settled, explain how to use alphabet free association stories for introductions. (3–4 minutes)

➤ Starting with the person whose first name begins with a letter closest to the beginning of the alphabet, introduce yourself to the group and read your story and its moral aloud.

➤ Continue in alphabetical order until everyone is introduced and has read their story.

5. When introductions are completed, invite participants to add to each other's stories.

➤ Exchange stories with someone in your group.

> Write a new happy ending or alternative moral to your partner's story.

> Or offer positive suggestions for coping with the dilemma presented in their story.

> After you have written comments on your partner's story, return it to its owner, retrieve your own story, and silently read your partner's additions to it.

6. Invite participants to share their new story.

> Quickly go around the group again, this time reading the alternative ending or moral advice you received from your partner.

7. Reconvene the large group and invite people to share pleasant surprises that emerged during alphabet free association. Encourage folks to remain open to personal associations during the workshop and to feel free to raise issues that pop up throughout the session.

Variations

▨ In work settings, ask participants to write about work-related stress or challenges.

▨ Tailor this exercise to the needs and interests of your group by asking participants to write a story about coping with specific issues that are important to the group (e.g., parenting, mental or physical health, balancing work and family, goal-setting, leadership, listening, problem solving, conflict resolution, values).

ALPHABET ASSOCIATIONS

A	N
B	O
C	P
D	Q
E	R
F	S
G	T
H	U
I	V
J	W
K	X
L	Y
M	Z

MY STORY

11 Good Person/Bad Person

In this introspective sequence of introductions, participants are asked to explore judgments they make about themselves.

Goals

To explore positive and negative beliefs about self.

To get acquainted.

Group size

Unlimited.

Time

15–20 minutes.

Materials

Optional: horn or harmonica for trainer's use as signal.

Process

☞ *This exercise has the potential to evoke strong emotions from some participants. Decide in advance what is appropriate for your audience and setting. For a lighthearted atmosphere, encourage participants to share some outrageous, humorous ways they are good or bad.*

1. Introduce the exercise with some comments appropriate to your group and goals about self-esteem, self-talk, and the judgments we all make about ourselves.

2. Announce that people will have a chance to get acquainted in a unique way by experimenting with sharing positive and negative judgments of themselves. Ask participants to find a partner.

➤ Everyone please stand up and find someone you don't know, who is either shorter or taller than you.

➤ Introduce yourselves and take a minute to get acquainted.

3. Once everyone is paired up and introduced, give instructions for the first good/bad exchange.

➤ For the next few minutes, the shorter person in each pair will assume the role of a **good boy** or **good girl**; the taller person will take on the **bad girl** or **bad boy** role.

➤ **Bad girls** and **bad boys** go first. Take 1 minute to tell your good girl or good boy partner why you are bad. You might, for example, believe you are bad because you don't call your parents often enough, don't exercise consistently, spend a lot of money on cars, binge on candy bars, don't pay bills on time, or leave dirty clothes on the floor.

➤ As quickly as you can, tell all the ways you are bad.

➤ Pay attention to what you choose to share. Do not disclose anything you don't want to.

➤ **Good boys** and **good girls,** listen without interrupting.

4. After 1–2 minutes, interrupt the conversations and invite the **good girls** and **good boys** to have their say.

➤ Now it's time for the **good girls** and **good boys** to tell the bad girls and bad boys all the ways you are good. You might, for example, believe you are good because you love your children, work hard, contribute to charity, believe in God, don't participate in gossip, keep yourself in good shape, or read to improve your mind.

➤ **Good** people, take 1 minute to quickly tell all the ways you are good.

5. After 1–2 minutes, interrupt discussions and invite participants to talk with their partners about what they learned about themselves in this exchange. (4 minutes)

➤ Take a few minutes to share your insights about positive or negative beliefs you have about yourself.

➤ Be sure your partner gets equal air time.

6. After 4–5 minutes, stop the discussions and give instructions for another round of good and bad introductions, this time with a small group. (8–10 minutes)

➤ Stay with your current partner and pair up with another twosome, creating a group of four people.

☞ *Be sure groups are settled before giving the next instructions. If there is an extra twosome, create one group of six and warn them they will have to be brief in the next round of introductions and discussion.*

➤ Before you introduce yourself in this group, switch roles. All the **good girls** and **good boys** are now bad, and the **bad boys** and **bad girls** are now good.

➤ Take turns introducing yourselves as good or bad, giving reasons why this is so.

➢ Go around the group, starting with the tallest person.

➢ Take about 2 minutes each for introducing your good or bad self.

➤ When everyone is introduced, take some time to discuss your insights about the effects of positive and negative judgments on yourself and others.

7. Reconvene the group and invite people to share insights and discoveries. Where possible, relate these responses to your next topic or learning objective.

Variations

▨ This exercise is especially appropriate for therapy, growth, and educational groups where people are exploring issues of self-esteem, identity, shame, pride, and self-acceptance.

▨ For work-related groups, have people identify the ways they think they are good and bad at their job.

12 Blue Ribbon

This affirming icebreaker can be used anytime, anywhere, for giving participants needed recognition, validation, and support.

Goals

To get acquainted by sharing positive achievements.

To recognize and affirm personal strengths.

Group size

Unlimited.

Time

5–10 minutes.

Materials

Blue Ribbon worksheets; several scissors; straight pins.

Process

1. Distribute **Blue Ribbon** worksheets with straight pins, and invite participants to prepare for introductions.

   ➤ Write your name in the center of your ribbon.

   ➤ Take a minute to reflect on your personal strengths and achievements. Where in your life do you deserve some blue ribbons (e.g., for single parenting, for biting your tongue when your partner tells the same joke for the fifth time, for sticking to your exercise routine, for volunteering your time as a scout leader)?

      ➤ On the streamers of the ribbon, write at least ten of the large and small accomplishments for which you deserve a blue ribbon.

   ➤ When finished, cut out your ribbon and pin it on your shoulder.

2. Invite participants to introduce themselves to the group by sharing blue ribbon achievements.

   ➤ Introduce yourself to the group by stating your first name and sharing the ten reasons you deserve a blue ribbon.

3. When introductions are finished, invite participants to wear their blue ribbons for the rest of the workshop or group session. Note that these name tags serve as a visible reminder of the strengths different people bring to the group.

Variations

■ In groups larger than 10–12 people, form into small groups of 6–8 people for introductions in Step 2. Try grouping people by state or county of birth or by favorite color.

■ In large workshop settings, invite people to mill around and get acquainted by reading each other's blue ribbon achievements as they introduce themselves by name and shake hands. Then form small groups for the public affirmation in Step 2. Carry out the state fair theme by designating names for the blue ribbon groups (e.g., jams, pickles, pies, pumpkins, sheep, quilts). For randomization of participants into groups, these group names could be written on the backs of the worksheets before they are distributed.

BLUE RIBBON

13 Analogies

These short, creative processes for getting acquainted use metaphors that are invariably funny and surprisingly meaningful: **Fruit Stand**, **Couch Potato**, and **Name That Tune**.

Goals

To warm-up to the topic.

To get to know other participants in a creative and playful way.

Group size

Unlimited.

Time

5–10 minutes.

Fruit Stand

1. Ask everyone to introduce themselves using a fruit as an analogy.
   ➤ Introduce yourself and tell what fruit best describes your expectations for this course or group session.

2. Summarize responses of the group, clarify questions about the agenda or group expectations, and move on to your first topic.

Variations

▨ For small groups, consider using an actual bowl of fresh fruit set in the center of the room, letting people keep the fruit they select for a snack later on in the session.

▨ For large groups, form smaller groups of 6–10 participants by their favorite fruit.

Couch Potato

1. Invite participants to introduce themselves by making a media comparison.

   ➤ Consider what type of TV program best characterizes you and your personality.

     ☞ *Be sure to give lots of examples (e.g., are you a situation comedy, quiz show, prime-time drama, cartoon, news report, infomercial, weather report, outdoor report, mystery, public service announcement, talk show, old movie, special event coverage, action/adventure, soap opera, sports competition, late night comedy, family entertainment special, documentary, or music video?).*

   ➤ Introduce yourself to the group, telling what type of TV show describes you best and why.

2. When introductions are finished, move on to the first topic for your group.

Variations

▧ For health and wellness groups, ask people to pick a TV program that represents their approaches to health or fitness.

▧ For introductions in a work-related group or with job-related content, invite participants to compare their leadership/management style or current workplace culture to a TV show.

Name That Tune

1. Ask participants to introduce themselves using a musical analogy appropriate to your session content.

     ☞ *Be sure to give several good examples: "Feeling Groovy," "Bridge Over Troubled Water," "Celebration," "Don't Worry, Be Happy."*

   ➤ What song title best describes your mood as we start this session?

     ➤ If you can't think of a real song title, make one up.

Variations

Tailor the musical analogy to your group, focus, and goals. Participants could select a song title that represents their current health status, stress management style, self-care patterns, life goals, stress on the job, philosophy of life, adolescence, marriage, approach to conflict, self-esteem, family rules, or any other topic that fits your learning objectives.

14 Name Games

Learning the names of other participants becomes easy and interesting in these three short name games: **Alphabet Neighbors**, **Athletic ABCs**, and **What's in a Name?**

Goals

To learn the names of other participants.

To get acquainted.

Group size

Unlimited.

Time

5–10 minutes.

Materials

What's in a Name?; newsprint or blackboard.

Alphabet Neighbors

☞ *This exercise works best with large groups (30 or more); group people by using different sections of the alphabet (e.g., A–E; F–M; N–Q; R–Z).*

1. Invite participants to create small groups by finding 5 or 6 other people whose first name begins with the same letter as theirs.

    ☞ *If any group is larger than 10 people, divide it in half. Combine groups with fewer than 5 people.*

2. Give instructions for introductions.

    ➤ Sit down in a circle with your alphabet companions.

    ➤ Learn the first name of everyone in your group.

    ➤ Each person introduce yourself.

➣ Then, practice saying everyone's name several times until everyone knows everyone else.

3. Interrupt after 3–4 minutes and invite each small group to make introductions to the entire group.

➤ Ask a member of your group to volunteer to introduce your group to other groups.

➣ If no one volunteers, the person with the most letters in their first name will make the introduction.

➤ When your turn comes, stand up and introduce each person in your group by first name. (e.g., We're the As: Alice, Alan, Arthur, Allie, and Adam; We're the Bs: Ben, Bob, Betty, Brenda, Bridgette, and Bessy).

☞ *Guide the process along quickly, moving from group to group in alphabetical order until everyone has been introduced.*

Variations

▦ If time allows, ask if anyone can remember the names of the alphabet neighbors in another group, then ask volunteers to test their memory by trying to repeat the names of a select group. For a silly prize, give the winner (who remembers the most names) a can of alphabet soup.

Athletic ABCs

1. Ask the group to brainstorm a list of athletic events from A to Z.

☞ *Move quickly through the alphabet, giving examples to get the ball rolling, and encouraging imaginative responses. The list on the next page provides a starting point.*

2. Invite participants to introduce themselves using athletic events as a catchy—and hopefully memorable—enhancement to their name.

➤ Introduce yourself by combining your first or last name with a sport or athletic event that begins with the same letter (e.g., John Ping-Pong Peterson, Skating Sally Brown).

➤ If you prefer, make up a new sport or athletic event to match your name (e.g., Fred Frog-Jumper Jones, Carla Computer-Disc-Thrower Goldman).

Athletic ABCs List

aerobics, archery, acrobatics
badminton, baseball, basketball, bowling, boxing
cricket, croquet, calisthenics, catch, curling, cheerleading
discus, dancing, dodgeball, diving
equestrian events
fencing, football, fox
geese, golf, gymnastics
handball, hockey, horseshoes, hurdles
ice skating, ice dancing
jockey, javelin, judo
kickball, karate
lacrosse, leap frog, lawn tennis
monkey in the middle
ninepins
Ping-Pong, polo, pole vaulting
roller skating, racing, rugby, rowing
skiing, soccer, softball, squash, swimming
tennis, table tennis, track and field, tumbling
umpiring
volleyball
water polo, wrestling, weight lifting
yoga

What's in a Name?

1. Distribute blank paper and invite people to reflect on their names.

➤ Write your responses to the following statements about your names.

© 1997 Whole Person Associates 210 W Michigan Duluth MN 55802-1908   800-247-6789

☞ *Write these statements on newsprint or a blackboard for easy reference by participants.*

➤ My full birth name is _____ .

➤ My middle name was chosen for me by _____ because _____ .

➤ My nickname _____ was given to me by _____ because _____ .

➤ My fantasy name or the name I would choose if I could change my name is _____ because _____ .

2. Give instructions for getting acquainted. (4–5 minutes)

➤ Introduce yourself to the group by reading your birth name and then sharing the rest of your name stories.

☞ *With groups of 10 or more, form several smaller groups that share simultaneously. Try grouping by vowels in first or last name and adjust creatively as needed until you have 6–8 people per group.*

Variations

▨ Distribute crayons and/or fine tip watercolor markers along with blank paper. Begin by asking people to make a graphic design of their name (first, last, both, or nickname). Allow about 5 minutes for this creative venture before proceeding to Step 1.

15 Short Stories

In these two brief get-acquainted processes, participants tell short stories about their life journey(**Journey**) and share special first experiences (**Firsts**).

Goals

To get acquainted with other group members.

To build trust and rapport.

Group size

Unlimited.

Time

10–15 minutes.

Materials

Journey: blackboard or newsprint; marker.

Firsts: horn or harmonica for signaling time to change partners.

Journey

1. Write the following quotations on newsprint or a blackboard:

   Life is a journey, not a destination.

   Hindsight is 20-20 vision.

2. Explain that participants will get acquainted by sharing reflections about their life journeys, using wisdom gained from hindsight. Give instructions for dividing into trios.

   ➤ Find two other people you don't know well who are wearing shoes similar to yours.

   ➤ Sit down facing each other and introduce yourselves.

3. When groups are settled, give instructions for reflection and sharing.
   - ➤ If you think about the past five years of your life as a journey, where were you departing from and what was your destination?
      - ☞ *Pause a moment for reflection here and after the next question.*
   - ➤ What did you learn along the way?
   - ➤ Each person has 3 minutes to share their story.
      - ➤ The person with the smallest shoe begins.
      - ➤ Ask someone to volunteer to be group timekeeper.
      - ➤ Listen to each other's stories without interrupting the speaker, except to ask for clarification if needed.
      - ☞ *Offer reminders about time limits, if needed, to keep groups moving along.*

4. Regather the large group. If time allows, invite participants to share pearls of wisdom gained from hindsight about their life journey, then relate these insights to the topic of the group.

Variations

▮ This process is easily adapted to other specific issues. Work groups could focus on career journeys instead of life journeys. Groups dealing with nutrition or eating disorders might explore participants' relationship with food.

Firsts

☞ *In this exercise people share in pairs, change partners several times, and share stories with up to five different people. As an alternative, have people share throughout in small groups of 4–6 people. Several groups can participate simultaneously.*

1. Introduce the exercise by asking participants to indicate by a show of hands how many people are participating in a group

such as this for the first time. Acknowledge the courage involved with *firsts* of any kind and, if applicable, share something that you are trying for the first time with this particular group or workshop.

2. Invite participants to get acquainted with other participants by sharing some of the *firsts* in their life.
   > Stand up and find a partner whom you do not know.
   > Introduce yourself and take turns responding to this statement: *The first time I purposely disobeyed my parents was . . .*
     > Each person has 1 minute to respond.
   > When you hear the horn or harmonica, find a new partner.
     ☞ *Keep time and blow the horn or harmonica after 2 minutes to signal time to change partners.*
   > Now find a new partner, introduce yourself, and take turns responding to this statement: *The first time I thought about death was . . .*

3. Guide the group through a series of three more partner changes and three additional *first* stories.
   > *The first time I questioned my values or did something that violated my sense of values was . . .*
   > *The first time I accomplished something on my own was . . .*
   > *The first time I felt responsible for some part of my well-being or self-care was . . .*

4. Reconvene the group and invite comments and observations, using these insights to make a bridge to your next agenda.

Variations
   ■ Adapt *first* statements to the specific issues or concerns of your audience (e.g., for health or wellness education groups: *the first time I became concerned about my health; the first time I experienced a sense of joy in movement*).

16 Fortunate Cookies

In this inspiring mood-setter, participants share their good fortunes.

Goals

To get acquainted.
To affirm personal resources and goals.

Time

10 minutes.

Materials

Fortunate Cookies worksheets.

Process

1. Hand out **Fortunate Cookies** worksheets and give instructions.
   > Looking back over your life, what do you consider your good fortunes?
   > In the space surrounding the cookie on your worksheet, list as many of your good fortunes as you can think of.

2. After 2–3 minutes, ask people to predict a possible fortune for their future.
   > Write a desirable fortune for your future inside your fortunate cookie.

3. Invite participants to get acquainted in trios.
   > Find two people you do not know well who look like they might bring you good fortune.
   > Sit down together, introduce yourselves, and take turns sharing your good fortunes and your fortune for the future.

4. Reconvene the group and invite participants to share examples of good fortunes they have had in life or will have in the future.

FORTUNATE COOKIES

Group Building

The twelve icebreakers in this section offer opportunities to combine specific content with creative processes that simultaneously build camaraderie, trust, and positive spirit in the group.

17 Match Up

Participants match puzzle pieces as an intriguing way to get acquainted with each other and the topic.

Goals

To meet other participants and build group camaraderie.

To get focused on the session content and pool group insights about the topic.

Group size

Unlimited. Works best with large groups.

Time

10–15 minutes.

Materials

For each small group of 4–6 people: one trainer-created jigsaw puzzle, prepared in advance and cut in four to six pieces; newsprint; markers; glue; masking tape.

Process

☞ *Prior to the workshop or group session create enough jigsaw puzzles and pieces to match your anticipated group size. Collect thematic visual images from magazines, newspapers, postcards, posters, computer graphics, product packaging, junk mail, catalogs, or placemats. Glue thin images onto cardboard before cutting them into four to six intriguingly-shaped pieces, according to the size of small groups you intend to form. Mix up all the pieces and put them in a box. Make an extra puzzle or two. Save these extras to mix in at the last minute if more people than you expect show up. This generic process can be easily adapted to nearly any subject (see*

*suggestions in the variations). As written, the icebreaker serves as
a general warm-up to a health-related topic.*

1. As participants arrive, have them draw a puzzle piece from the box. Give a brief welcome and orientation to the goals and learning objectives of the session.

2. Invite participants to pull out the puzzle piece they received on arrival and give instructions for getting matched up in groups. (2–3 minutes)

   ➤ Your puzzle piece is one of several that can be matched up to make a picture of something related to our topic.

   ➤ Your task is to find all the missing pieces to your puzzle.

      ➤ Stand up and walk around the room, comparing pieces with other people.

      ➤ When you find someone with a matching piece, introduce yourself, then work as a team to find other matching pieces.

   ➤ When you have your puzzle all put together, find a place to sit down together with your group.

3. As groups get matched up, distribute markers, glue or tape, and scissors to each group. When all groups are settled and equipped, give instructions for brainstorming health tips. (4 minutes)

   ➤ Start by taping or gluing your completed puzzle picture at the top of your newsprint.

   ➤ Then, together as a group, brainstorm health tips related to your picture.

      ➤ Write your list of health tips on the newsprint below your picture.

      ➤ You have 4 minutes to make a list of at least ten health tips.

4. When 4 minutes have passed, go around the room and ask a

spokesperson from each group to stand up, show their puzzle picture, and read the ten health tips related to their picture.

☞ *Give examples of tips using an image that is different from those the groups have (e.g., a picture puzzle of a running shoe might inspire tips such as the following: wear shoes that fit; pace yourself; exercise moderately; start slowly and build up gradually to more speed or distance; run with a partner for support).*

5. Use the tips generated in this process to set your agenda and make bridges to content areas covered during the rest of the session.

Variations

▪ To provide a rich backdrop for learning, ask groups to hang their posters with health tips around the room.

▪ By changing the nature of the picture puzzles, you can easily adapt this exercise to most groups. Relaxation groups might be given pictures of peaceful scenes like a sunset or a person sleeping in bed. Health education groups might receive pictures of junk food, a pack of cigarettes, an ad for liquor, or walking shoes. Groups focused on relationships could piece together puzzle pictures showing families, couples, leisure activities, or scenes of potential conflict.

▪ In Step 3 have groups brainstorm tips appropriate to specific learning objectives (e.g., tips for relaxation, better eating, stopping smoking, sticking to an exercise program, playful intimacy, positive communication, conflict resolution).

18 Wheel of Fortune

This face-paced icebreaker gives participants an opportunity to share wellness attitudes with a succession of group members as they follow the wheel of fortune's spin.

Goals

To promote self-disclosure and interaction among participants.

To consider attitudes and experiences related to wellness.

Group size

Unlimited, as long as there is plenty of open space to make the Wheel of Fortune.

Time

10–15 minutes.

Materials

Topic-specific **Conversation Starters** handout prepared in advance by the trainer (see list of suggestions on page 60; make sure the starters are numbered); microphone (for groups of 30 or more people); whistle, bell, or harmonica to signal partner changes.

Process

1. Ask participants to pair up with a neighbor and introduce themselves by briefly telling each other about a favorite card game or board game from childhood. (2 minutes)

2. After 2 minutes, interrupt and instruct pairs to decide who will be the **Poker Chip** and who will be the **Silver Dollar.**

3. Give instructions for making the Wheel of Fortune.
   ➤ **Silver Dollars,** form a circle in the middle of the room with your backs to the center of the circle.

> **Poker Chips,** stand facing your partners, forming a larger circle on the outside of the Silver Dollars.

4. As participants are getting into position, distribute **Conversation Starter** handouts.

5. When everyone is in place, instruct **Poker Chips** to move one person to their left so that everyone is facing a new partner.

6. Choose a nonthreatening conversation starter from the handout and call out the number. Instruct participants to respond by sharing their answers with their partner.
   > Each person has 30 seconds to respond to the conversation starter. Make sure your partner gets equal time.
   > I will keep time and let you know when 1 minute is up.

7. Instruct each **Poker Chip** to move one person to the left again, then call out the number of any other conversation starter.
   > Each person has 30 seconds to respond to the conversation starter.

8. Repeat Step 7 several times until the group is warmed up to the subject and each other. Choose conversation starters that apply to the theme of the session. Feel free to add humorous or serious ideas that are pertinent to your audience.

Variations

▦ Instead of forming pairs, form groups of 4–8 people. When you call a number, group members take turns responding to the conversation starter. Allow several members to respond to a given conversation starter before calling another number. When you call another number, the next group member responds to the new conversation starter. Continue this process, keeping the pace moving quickly until your time is up.

▦ Substitute topical conversation starters geared to your group and goals.

CONVERSATION STARTERS

1. My favorite cartoon or comic strip is . . .
2. If I changed jobs . . .
3. If I could change one thing in the environment I would . . .
4. If I could give up one bad habit . . .
5. Life . . .
6. The most important thing in my life . . .
7. If I had only 6 months to live . . .
8. Healthy foods . . .
9. To take better care of myself I should . . .
10. The best thing about life is . . .
11. The worst things about life is . . .
12. If my body could speak . . .
13. The part of my body where I collect tension . . .
14. Don't ever tease me about . . .
15. Five years from now . . .
16. The most important thing I can do to improve my health . . .
17. The best measure of health . . .
18. When I get sick . . .
19. Happiness is . . .
20. Health is . . .
21. Wellness is . . .
22. Illness is . . .
23. When I get a cold, I . . .
24. When it comes to health, I feel responsible for . . .
25. My doctor . . .
26. One thing I have difficulty accepting about myself . . .
27. I am critical of myself when . . .
28. When I'm under stress . . .
29. Exercise . . .
30. When I'm angry . . .

Thanks to Sandy Queen, Director of Lifeworks and author of Wellness Activities for Youth, *whose enormous contributions to health education include this list of conversation starters.*

19 Course Application Form

Nothing enhances involvement in a group more than a personal campaign to be included as a participant.

Goals

To enhance personal and group motivation for learning.

To promote group collaboration, support, and trust.

Group size

Unlimited.

Time

5–10 minutes.

Materials

Gold stars; **Course Application Form** worksheets.

Process

☞ *Bring plenty of gold stars so that participants can have a number to give away to other participants.*

1. Give everyone a **Course Application Form**, then tell participants that you want them to apply for admission into the (session/course/workshop) by identifying personal needs and motivations for taking the course. (2–3 minutes)

   ➤ Write your name and the course title on the top of your application form in the spaces provided.

   ➤ Now list several reasons why you need this course right now. What are your reasons for attending?.

     ☞ *Give examples that might typically fit your audience and themes (e.g., I'm stuck in a rut of all work and no play; my doctor said I need to reduce stress to stay healthy; I'm a single parent of three teenagers and need some ideas about parenting). Pause long enough for everyone to identify and record their needs.*

➤ Now shift your focus a bit. Imagine that space in the course is limited. Why should you, among all these applicants, be selected for this course?

   ➤ Don't be bashful or humble, on your application form write all the reasons why you should be selected.

   ☞ *Prime the pump with a few examples (e.g., I'm highly motivated for change or learning; I'm accepting and not judgmental of others; I am a good listener; I can raise interesting questions and will challenge the instructor if needed).*

2. Give everyone a generous supply of gold stars, then explain how participants should campaign to be included in the course on the basis of their needs and motivations. (5–6 minutes)

   ➤ During the next few minutes everyone will be campaigning with other participants, getting acquainted as you try to convince each other that you should be admitted.

      ➤ Each person will be wearing two different hats: **course applicant** and **course approver**.

   ➤ As a **course applicant,** campaign to be included on the basis on your needs and motivations.

      ➤ Move around the room, introduce yourself to other participants, and try to persuade folks that you are a good candidate for this course.

      ➤ Share your needs and motivations and make a convincing case for your acceptance into the course.

      ➤ Your goal is to collect as many gold stars of acceptance as you can in 5 minutes.

   ➤ As a **course approver,** listen to other course applicants' needs and motivations, and when you are convinced they should be accepted, put a gold star on their application.

> You can give more than one star if you want—two stars for *need* if you believe their need is strong, three stars for *motivation* if you think their motivation is very high.

☞ *Encourage folks to move quickly, pair up with several partners, and try to talk with at least three different people in the time allotted.*

3. Interrupt discussions and inquire if everyone has been accepted into the course.

☞ *If there are any folks who have not yet received stars of acceptance, give them stars now and affirm them for coming.*

4. Announce clearly that everyone has now been accepted into the course and give all participants a warm welcome. Then proceed with your orientation or first content segment.

Variations

▪ Counseling groups can modify the Course Application to a *Group* Application or *Treatment* Application.

▪ Add another category to the course applications form: **Recommendations. Course approvers** can write recommendations at the bottom of other participants' application forms (e.g., lower personal expectations and let yourself make a few mistakes; give yourself time to get to know other participants and feel comfortable in the group).

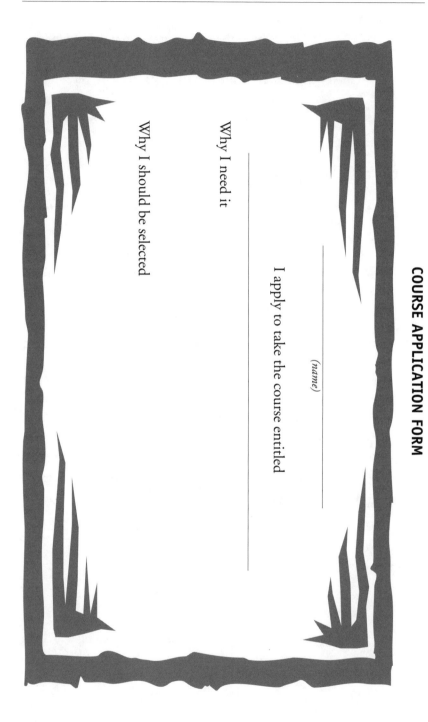

COURSE APPLICATION FORM

I apply to take the course entitled

_____

(name)

Why I need it

Why I should be selected

20 Natural Resources

This inspiring exercise affirms the natural wisdom and experience of each person and highlights the collective strengths of all participants.

Goals

To appreciate personal and group resources and the potential for growth.

To build a positive group atmosphere.

Group size

Unlimited.

Time

10–15 minutes.

Materials

Natural Resources worksheets; large sheet of butcher paper with a pine tree drawn on it; masking tape.

Process

☞ *Before participants arrive, hang the drawing of the pine tree on a wall or blackboard.*

1. Start by acknowledging that each person brings unique talents and abilities to the group and that you will begin by having everyone identify their own natural resources.

2. Hand out **Natural Resources** worksheets and ask people to reflect on their natural abilities and strengths. (3–4 minutes)

   ➤ Think about all the personal resources you bring with you today: your experience, background, abilities, knowledge, training, talents, virtues, strengths, attitudes, ingenuity, and resourcefulness.

> ➣ Consider your best qualities, skills, and life experiences. Perhaps you have survived divorce or other adversity, are a skilled negotiator, a trained nurse, or an experienced camper. Maybe you have raised children, started a business, or created a work of art. Or you may have a high level of wellness and physical energy.

> ➣ Write as many of your natural resources as you can think of on your worksheet.

> ➣ Don't be modest; claim *all* your strengths.

3. Invite participants to share their resources with another group member.

> ➣ Stand up and find a partner you do not already know.

> ➣ Take turns introducing yourselves and sharing your natural resources.

> ➣ Each person has 1 minute to share.

4. Interrupt after 2 minutes and invite partners to introduce each other to the large group. (4–5 minutes)

> ☞ *With groups of more than 20 participants, create small groups of 6–8 for introductions, using favorite types of trees to divide into groups.*

> ➣ Write the first name of your partner across the top of their worksheet.

> ➣ Come to the front of the room and introduce your partner by giving their first name, reading some of the resources they bring, and hanging their resource worksheet on the pine tree.

> ➣ After you have introduced your partner and have been introduced yourself, return to your seat and listen to introductions of other participants.

5. When everyone has been introduced and each person's resources have been added to the pine tree, ask participants to share observations about the collective natural resources of the group. Summarize common strengths.

6. Describe the tree as a metaphor for the strength of the group and give examples of how the resources of everyone present will enrich the group and help achieve personal or group goals.

Variations

■ For groups with easy access to woods, lakes, or other natural settings, consider asking people to go outdoors on a short scavenger hunt for a small natural object symbolizing their personal strength or ability. Use the objects for introductions and, when finished, display all the objects on a table.

NATURAL RESOURCES

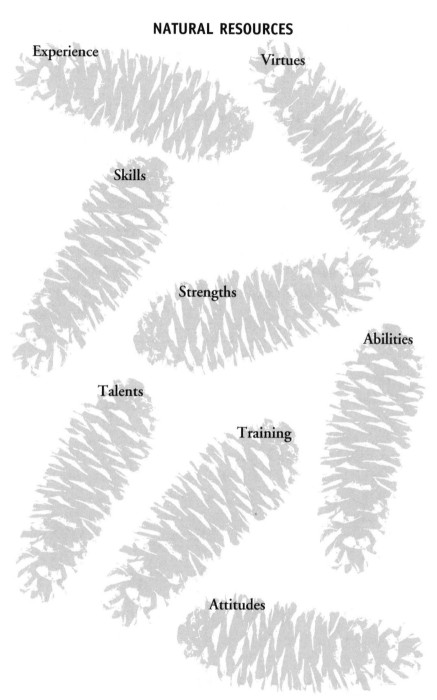

Experience

Virtues

Skills

Strengths

Abilities

Talents

Training

Attitudes

21 Birthday Signs

In this intriguing exercise, people discover what they have in common with other participants who share the same birthday sign.

Goals

To get acquainted.

To identify positive, health-enhancing qualities of people born under each astrological sign.

Group size

Unlimited.

Time

10–15 minutes.

Materials

Newsprint; markers; masking tape.

Process

1. Ask participants to divide into small groups according to their astrological birth sign: **Aries** (March 21–April 19); **Taurus** (April 20–May 20); **Gemini** (May 21–June 21); **Cancer** (June 22–July 22); **Leo** (July 23–August 22); **Virgo** (August 23–September 22); **Libra** (September 23–October 23); **Scorpio** (October 24–November 21); **Sagittarius** (November 22–December 21); **Capricorn** (December 22–January 19); **Aquarius** (January 20–February 18); **Pisces** (February 19–March 20).

   ☞ *Designate twelve areas of the room for the different astrological groups to gather.*

© 1997 Whole Person Associates 210 W Michigan Duluth MN 55802-1908   800-247-6789

2. Give each group newsprint and markers, then encourage folks
   to discover what they have in common with people who share
   their sign. (4–5 minutes)
   ➤ Take turns introducing yourselves and sharing examples of
      your personality traits. For example, you might say, "I'm
      Jim and I'm persistent, hard-working, loyal, romantic, and
      shy."
      ➤ Start with the person whose birthday comes first in your
         sign.
      ➤ Each person has 1 minute to share.
      ➤ Listen for traits you have in common with other people
         in your group.
   ➤ Ask someone to volunteer as reporter to take notes for your
      group.
      ➤ Reporters, write your group's birth sign at the top of the
         newsprint. Then divide the paper into two vertical col-
         umns. Label the left column **traits in common.**
   ➤ As people talk about their personality traits, listen for traits
      people in your group have in common with each other.
      ➤ In the left column, list personality traits that are men-
         tioned by more than one person in your group.
      ➤ If a trait is mentioned several times by different people,
         add a star each time it is mentioned.

3. After about 5 minutes, interrupt group discussions and instruct people to consider possible, health-enhancing qualities
   of people born under their sign. (3 minutes)
   ➤ Take a few minutes to brainstorm together some of the
      positive qualities of people born under your sign—quali-
      ties that enhance whole-person health or well-being.
   ➤ Reporters, list these qualities on the right side of your
      newsprint under the heading **positive, health-enhancing
      qualities.**

© 1997 Whole Person Associates 210 W Michigan Duluth MN 55802-1908   800-247-6789

4. Invite the reporter of each birth sign group in turn to introduce their group and share their discoveries with the large group.

5. When group introductions are finished, post the trait lists around the room. Select a few health-enhancing traits to use as content bridges to your next topic or learning objective.

Variations

■ Work groups could modify Step 3 to identify qualities which enhance work performance, productivity, or teamwork.

■ In a longer session or workshop, encourage people to use break times to discover commonalities with people born under other signs. Just before the break, remind participants to pair up with someone born under a different sign. After the break, ask for a few examples of personality traits people found they had in common despite their differences.

© 1997 Whole Person Associates 210 W Michigan Duluth MN 55802-1908   800-247-6789

22 Uncommon Commonalties

Hilarious connections and good-humored bonding result when participants discover the most unusual thing they have in common.

Goals

To discover unique commonalties with other participants.

To feel connected with another group member and the group as a whole.

Group size

Unlimited.

Time

5–10 minutes.

Process

1. Begin with a few comments on the importance of having common goals for the learning experience. Affirm the value of connecting with others to discover what we have in common.

2. Invite participants to make a connection with one other person in the group. (3–4 minutes)

   ➤ Pair up with someone you do not know well.

   ➤ Take a few minutes to get acquainted by finding out what you have in common with each other.

   ☞ *Pause for 2 minutes.*

   ➤ Now decide together what is the most unusual thing you have in common with each other.

3. Invite pairs to share their uncommon commonalities with the large group. (2–3 minutes)

   ☞ *With big groups, divide in half or thirds for sharing and then solicit the "most unusual" commonality from each group for the next step.*

4. Using an informal applause meter, ask the audience to vote on the most unusual commonality in the group. (1–2 minutes)

5. Congratulate the winning pair and give the group feedback on what you noticed they all had in common during the process (e.g., openness to a new idea, adventurous spirit, willingness to take risks, sense of humor, supportive attitude).

Thanks to Bob Czimbal for this intriguing process.

23 On Stage

This lively opener sets the stage for creativity, camaraderie, and comedy as supportive tools for exploring personal stress and coping alternatives.

Goals

To find things in common with other participants.

To approach a sensitive subject with a lighthearted and positive mindset.

Group size

Works best with groups of 20 or more people, as long as there is ample space for people to move around freely.

Time

20 minutes.

Materials

Blank paper.

Process

1. Distribute blank paper and ask participants to identify some of the stresses in their life and how they manage them.

> Take a minute to focus on the stress in your life recently.

> Make a list of at least ten major or minor stresses you've experienced recently.

☞ *Give lots of examples of big and small stress to help people get started (e.g., weather, divorce, job conflicts, politics, health concerns, hassles with children, expectations of extended family, loneliness, changes, disappointments, financial worries). Be sure everyone has listed ten or more before asking about coping strategies.*

➤ Now go back and reflect on how you've been coping with
each of these stresses.

➤ Jot down the positive and negative ways you've used to
deal with each stress.

☞ *Give some serious and humorous examples to get people*
thinking (e.g., avoidance, assertiveness, pouting, kick-
ing the dog, relaxation techniques, problem-solving,
getting drunk, placating, time management, smoking,
talking it over with a friend).

2. Ask participants to form small groups of 5–6 people.

➤ Find 4 or 5 other people who have used a coping strategy
similar to one or more on your list.

➤ When you have a group of 5 or 6, stake out some territory
in the room, sit down together, and introduce yourselves
briefly.

3. When groups are settled, invite participants to get acquainted
with each other—and the topic (10 minutes)

➤ Take turns sharing your stress lists.

➤ You have 5 minutes. Make sure everyone gets a turn.

☞ *Keep time and monitor the progress of groups, encour-*
aging people to keep the pace moving so everyone gets
a chance to talk about their stress. Interrupt after 5
minutes.

➤ Now that everyone has talked about their list, decide on one
stress you have in common and discuss the best ways to
cope with that stress.

4. Interrupt after 5 minutes and give instructions for the creative
segment. (6 minutes)

➤ Prepare a short skit that illustrates the stress you have in
common and demonstrates three or more strategies for
managing it.

➤ The skit should be no longer than 1 minute.

➤ Everyone in your group needs to participate.

☞ *Some people may cringe and groan at this assignment. Suggest those who detest such performances could act as MC for their group or provide sound effects.*

➤ You have 6 minutes to create your skit and be ready to perform it for the large group.

➤ Work quickly and have fun.

☞ *Remind participants when there are about 2 minutes left and it's time to wrap up their skit rehearsals. Reassure folks that nobody is expecting perfect, award-winning performances and it's okay to make mistakes, be silly, and—hopefully—have fun.*

5. After 6–8 minutes, announce that it's show time. Invite each group to perform their skit in the front of the room, then introduce each other when finished. Lead the group in applause for each group performance.

☞ *Keep the process moving along quickly.*

6. Thank each group for their stellar performance, then weave themes from the skits into the workshop.

Variations

▨ Instead of skits, ask participants to make up song lyrics expressing their common stress, set them to music, and perform the song for the group.

▨ Adapt this process to the content of your workshop by changing the themes for sharing and skit-making (e.g., work stress and coping, positive and problematic dynamics in families or other systems, leadership styles and pitfalls, communication skills, conflict management, self-care habits).

Thanks to Sandy Queen, Director of Lifeworks and author of Wellness Activities for Youth, *for sowing the seeds for this icebreaker.*

24 It's Catching!

This hilarious game will loosen up any group and bring fun and laughter to nearly any topic.

Goals

To relax and have fun.

To get energized.

Group size

Unlimited.

Time

5–10 minutes.

Process

1. Instruct participants to sit in a circle facing each other so they all can see each other.

   ☞ *If your group is larger than 20, form several small groups of 8–10 people. Try using the scissors, paper, rock game to divide up. On the count of three, everyone makes the symbol of scissors (two fingers extended); paper (flat palm outstretched); or rock (clenched fist). Participants find 8 others who have chosen the same symbol.*

2. Explain how the game works, giving a brief demonstration so everyone understands the process, and then play several rounds of this contagious game.

   ➤ In this game everyone will introduce themselves by giving their name and demonstrating some imaginary ailment that they are going to pass on to everyone else.

   ➤ The shortest person in the group begins.

> Say your name clearly and then describe your imaginary ailment and demonstrate it for the group.

   ☞ *Give several examples to spark creativity in the group (e.g., I have whooping cough; I'm paralyzed; My right eye is twitching).*

> Once the ailment is demonstrated, everyone else in the group should "catch" the ailment by mimicking the symptom.

> As soon as everyone has "caught" the symptom, the person to the left takes a turn using a different contagious introduction.

   > Everyone "catches" this new ailment while still continuing to suffer from the first.

> Continue around the group, each person making an introduction and succumbing to a new ailment, which is caught in turn by everyone else and added to all the other symptoms they already are experiencing.

   ☞ *By this time everyone should be jumping, twitching, coughing, sneezing, and having a great time. For double laughs, have someone film the activity and show it to the group later.*

Variations

▦ Tailor this exercise to your group and desired learning outcomes. For stress management workshops, ask participants to develop ailments that are physical manifestations of stress (e.g., drumming fingers, tense shoulders, the jitters, nervous cough, a scowl or frown, clenched fists, stuttering, facial tics). In listening skills training, focus on bad listening habits (e.g., poor eye contact, closed body posture, inattention, interrupting, fidgeting, looking bored).

25 Half or Half?

In this novel approach to getting acquainted, participants share optimistic and pessimistic perspectives on life.

Goals

To reflect on personal attitude, philosophy, and perspective on life.

To get to know other participants.

Group size

Unlimited.

Time

5–10 minutes.

Materials

Half or Half? worksheets.

Process

1. Invite participants to reflect on their typical perspective on life. Are they typically optimists or pessimists? Poll the group by a show of hands to see the balance.

   ☞ *If time allows, ask participants to form a human continuum along one wall. Designate one corner as "cynical pessimist" and the other corner as "cockeyed optimist." Invite people to stand and take their typical place on the continuum between these two extremes. Neighbors could discuss what went into their choice of position.*

2. Distribute **Half or Half?** worksheets and guide participants through a short reflection about their typical perspective on life. (4 minutes)

☞ *Allow ample time for reflection after each question.*

➤ As you look at the glass on your worksheet, would you typically think of it as half empty or half full?

  ➤ Write your typical perspective on your worksheet.

➤ What are some of the more joyful and positive experiences of your life? Perhaps you had a loving family, a college education, a good relationship with your partner, happy children, a well-paying job, or good health.

  ➤ In the bottom half of your glass, write some of the positive, affirming life experiences you can celebrate.

➤ What kinds of disappointments have you experienced in life? Perhaps you had an unhappy childhood, obstacles and barriers in your career, a troubled marriage, financial setbacks, or health concerns.

  ➤ Write some of your disappointing life experiences in the top half of your glass.

3. When most participants have finished their reflections, ask them to get acquainted with each other by sharing their typical perspectives.

  ➤ Pair up with someone you do not know well.

  ➤ Introduce yourself, then tell your partner whether you typically see the glass as half empty or half full.

    ➤ Without going into specific details about your joys and disappointments, tell why you think of yourself as an optimist or a pessimist.

  ➤ Each person has 1 minute to share.

4. After 2 minutes, interrupt discussions and instruct participants to find a new partner. When everyone is paired up, give the next instructions.

  ➤ Take turns sharing joyful, celebratory, affirming life experiences from the bottom half of your glass.

    ➤ Share only as much as feels comfortable.

> Each person has 1 minute to share.

5. Interrupt after 2 minutes and invite participants to find another new partner.

> Share whatever you'd like about the disappointing life experiences listed in the top half of your glass.

> Take turns.

> Each person has 1 minute to share.

6. Ask everyone to return to their seats, then invite participants to share thoughts and feelings raised by this activity. If time allows, lead a short discussion about how perceptions and life perspective can change under different circumstances.

Variations

This would be an interesting exercise to use with employees as a subjective measure of job satisfaction.

Families could use the glass image to explore levels of nurturing, affection, communication, and self-esteem.

The glass could be used by groups exploring individual levels of confidence, self-esteem, self-acceptance, body image, spiritual hunger, physical health, emotional serenity, healthy relationships, or social support.

© 1997 Whole Person Associates 210 W Michigan Duluth MN 55802-1908   800-247-6789

HALF OR HALF?

This glass is ❑ half empty
                ❑ half full

26 Mystery Feelings

This fascinating exercise engages participants in personal sharing
that is playful, nonthreatening, and potentially helpful for identifying feelings.

Goals

To share feelings in a playful, nonthreatening way.

To get acquainted informally and warm up to the group.

Group size

Unlimited.

Time

5–10 minutes.

Materials

Feeling word label for each participant. Prepare labels in advance
using computer address labels or others of similar size. Write a
different feeling word on each label. Print clearly in large letters
and be sure to include a wide variety of different feelings (e.g.,
*angry, annoyed, irritated, frustrated, sad, scared, anxious, worried,
panicky, confused, happy, excited, calm, peaceful, bored, relieved,
disappointed, hurt*).

Process

1. Announce that participants will get acquainted by playing a
   short guessing game using a variety of mystery feelings. Caution participants not to reveal other people's mystery feeling
   words or peek at their own. Then go around the group and put
   a feeling label on the forehead of each person.

   ☞*In a large group, ask for assistance in distributing labels. If anyone objects to putting the label on their forehead, ask to stick it out of sight on their shoulder or back.*

2. Ask participants to arrange their chairs in a circle or in several circles of 6–7 people if your group is large. Then explain how the mystery feeling game works.

➤ Someone volunteer to go first.

    ➣ You are the great detective **Sherlock Holmes**.

    ➣ Your task is to try to guess the mystery feeling written on your forehead.

➤ Other group members, you are **Watsons**. One at a time, give Sherlock clues by giving examples of when you last felt this feeling or by identifying circumstances that trigger this feeling in you.

    ☞ *Give several pertinent examples (e.g., I last felt this feeling when my son was two hours late coming home and did not call me; I feel this way when a friend forgets an appointment with me).*

➤ **Sherlock,** you have one guess for each example given by each Watson in your group.

    ➣ To identify the feeling correctly and solve the mystery, you must guess the exact feeling word written on your forehead label.

      ☞ *Clarify by giving several examples. If the word is anger, the words irritated or annoyed are not acceptable. Sherlock must guess the word anger. Excitement is different from happiness or nervousness or eagerness.*

    ➣ If Sherlock does not guess the mystery feeling after the first clue, the second **Watson** offers a new example or clue, based on personal experience with this feeling.

➤ Continue around the circle, offering clues and guesses until Sherlock guesses the feeling or until each Watson has offered a clue.

© 1997 Whole Person Associates 210 W Michigan Duluth MN 55802-1908   800-247-6789

> If everyone has given a clue and Sherlock still cannot figure out the feeling, the group should reveal the mystery feeling to Sherlock.

> Take turns playing the role of Sherlock so that everyone has an opportunity to identify their mystery feeling.

3. Reconvene the group and ask people what they learned from the mystery feeling game. Summarize common experiences, respond to issues raised, and relate feeling identification to the group goals and upcoming topics.

Variations

Relate feelings to specific issues or topics of your group by asking participants to use examples relevant to your audience (e.g., feelings associated with parenting experiences, gay and lesbian issues, balancing work and family, managing stress, on-the-job conflicts).

© 1997 Whole Person Associates 210 W Michigan Duluth MN 55802-1908   800-247-6789

27 Master/Servant

When participants implement the dynamics of power to create a positive group climate, the results are surprising, delightful, and energizing.

Goals

To experience the beneficial effects of using power.

To build group spirit and promote positive energy.

Group size

Unlimited. Works best with large groups.

Time

5–10 minutes.

Process

1. Instruct people to form quartets by finding 3 other people who are close to their height.

2. When everyone has joined a group, give instructions for using power dynamics to create joy and celebration.

   ➤ The person with the most quarters in their pocket or purse is **master;** the other three group members are **servants.**

   ➤ **Masters,** you have absolute power over your servants, but you must use your power only to promote joy, celebration, and positive spirit among them and with the rest of the groups.

      ➤ **Masters,** take a minute to think of something positive your servants could do that would promote joy, laughter, celebration, well-being, vitality, peace, calm, or confidence for people in the room. They will have about 3 minutes to accomplish the task.

> When you have a creative idea in mind, give your servants their instructions.

➤ **Servants,** your responsibility is to carry out your master's instructions quickly and eagerly.

> As soon as you receive your instructions, circulate around the room for 3 minutes fulfilling your servant role.

> When you approach another person or group, explain your master's instructions and then carry them out as ordered.

☞ *Give lots of creative example (e.g., My master says to smile at you, give you a hug, give you a compliment, rub your shoulders, sing you a lullaby).*

3. When 3 minutes are up, reconvene the group and compliment masters and servants for creating such a positive atmosphere for learning.

Variations

▪ Consider changing the words master and servant to words better suited to your audience or setting: for work settings, substitute **boss** and **workers** or **supervisor** and **employees.** Other ideas are **ruler** and **subjects, commander** and **troops, captain** and **crew, leader** and **followers, honcho** and **peons.**

▪ To look at the dynamics of power in more depth, repeat this process several times so that everyone has an opportunity to be in the position of power. Then ask quartets to share their experience with power in this setting and formulate a list of ten dynamics of power.

Thanks to Krysta Kavanaugh, editor of Marriage *magazine, and Matt Weinstein, author of* Playfair, *who introduced us to this powerful technique.*

28 Classified

In this creative activity, participants write a positive want ad for someone they have difficulty appreciating.

Goals

To demonstrate that everyone, including difficult people, has qualities and strengths worth appreciating.

To change negative attitudes into positive, accepting ones.

Group size

Unlimited.

Time

5–10 minutes.

Materials

Blank paper.

Process

1. Poll the group to determine who experiences stress resulting from a conflict or difficulty with someone at work, at home, or in any other area of life.

    ☞ *If all hands don't go up, playfully chide the resisters, asking if they don't at least have a surly bus driver or meddling relative they have difficulty with.*

2. Announce that participants will have an opportunity to relieve some of that stress in an unusual way. Reinforce the point that all of us have people in our lives that may be difficult to appreciate. Then distribute blank paper and guide people through the imagery and reflection process. (5 minutes)

    ☞ *Don't rush! Pause long enough between each instruction so*

> *that people have time to form the mental images and consider their responses. Remember, they don't know the script.*

➤ Close your eyes and think about a person that you have difficulty relating to—perhaps a colleague, a supervisor, a neighbor, or a family member. *(Pause)*

➤ Why is it so hard for you to relate to this person? What gets in your way? *(Pause)*

➤ Now shift your focus slightly to consider some more positive qualities this person has. Try to appreciate the uniqueness and strength of this individual.

> ➤ How could you restate some of the negatives you see as positive attributes or qualities?

> ➤ What are some strong points of this person?

> ➤ What special gifts does this person bring to your job or family?

> ➤ What are the benefits of working or living with this person?

➤ Now pretend that this person is placing a want ad, looking for a new job or family. Keeping this person's positive qualities in mind, your job is to write a classified ad focusing on the benefits of working or living with this person.

> ➤ Use only positive statements to describe qualities you and others might appreciate about this person.

> ☞ *Offer a few sample classifieds to help stimulate creative thinking:*

> *Teenage boy looking for family. Bright, verbal, quick to respond to challenges from authority. Willing to try anything. Funny, outrageous, guaranteed to make you laugh and keep your life interesting. Call 734-8899 for more information.*

> *Loyal and tidy office assistant looking for work setting where finishing projects on time is a top priority.*

3. When everyone has a classified ready, invite participants to share their want ads with the group.

☞ *With groups larger than 12 people, use favorite comic strips to form smaller groups of 8–12 for the public readings.*

➤ Take turns reading your ads to the group.

➤ Make an effort to be totally convincing as you extol the virtues of this person to the group.

4. Solicit observations about what participants learned from making a want ad for their chosen person. End the discussion with a gentle reminder: *People will behave as they are expected to behave.*

Variations

▨ Instead of a classified ad, participants could design a poster based on the strengths of the person.

Thanks to Randy Weigel, PhD, University of Wyoming, for this creative concept.

Self-Awareness

The eleven icebreakers in this section offer intriguing processes for self discovery that involve taking stock and taking charge.

29 Alarm Clocks

Participants identify the type of wake-up calls they receive when they are experiencing stress.

Goals

To discover personal signals of stress.

To raise self-awareness and promote self-care.

Group size

Unlimited.

Time

5–10 minutes.

Materials

Alarm Clocks worksheets.

Process

1. Set the stage for this brief self-assessment by giving a short chalktalk about the connection between self-care and self-awareness.

   ● **Self-care depends on holistic self-awareness.** Taking good care of yourself requires awareness and understanding of how you are—how you function, how you feel, how you get along in the world. This requires observing yourself, listening to yourself, and noticing when things are not right with you—when your body, mind, emotions, spirit, or relationships are out of balance.

2. Hand out **Alarm Clocks** worksheets and invite participant to reflect on their personal signals of stress. (5 minutes)

➤ Each of you has your own alarm clocks or personal signals
of stress.

➤ When you are under stress and something has gotten out
of balance—in your body, mind, emotions, spirit, or relationships—your alarm will go off.

➤ What are your personal alarms or signals of stress?

  ➤ Do you receive an SOS from your *body* by getting head-
aches, stomach aches, insomnia, fatigue, skin rashes, or
respiratory infections?

  ➤ Does your *mind* signal you've had enough by poor
concentration, forgetfulness, avoidance of new learning opportunities, or lack of creativity?

  ➤ When your *emotional* alarms go off, are you feeling depressed, angry, anxious, frustrated, lonely, or abandoned?

  ➤ Do you receive *spiritual* alarms such as loss of purpose,
faith, or serenity, or an increase in anger and resentment
and the inability to forgive and move on with your life?

  ➤ What are your *relationship* alarms? Do you have a lot
more arguments with your partner when you are stress?
Do you withdraw and isolate yourself or get yourself
overcommitted and then feel overwhelmed and resent-
ful toward people?

➤ Write your personal signals of stress on your alarm clock.

  ➤ Try to think of alarms for each area of your life: body,
mind, emotions, spirit, and relationships.

3. Invite participants to share examples of personal signals of
stress, concluding with a reminder that self-care involves pay-
ing attention to personal alarm clocks and using these signals
as a catalyst for increased self-care.

Variations

■ This exercise can be adapted to the specific interests or concerns of your audience by changing alarm signals from signals of *stress* to signals of something else (e.g., *anger* or *the risk of being abusive* for people with anger and abuse problems; *family stress*—ask everyone in the family to create a family alarm clock; symptoms of *addiction* or *relapse*).

ALARM CLOCKS

Body

Mind

Emotions

Spirit

Relationships

30 Goldfish Bowl

When participants share vulnerabilities in this simple, nonthreatening exercise, group trust and intimacy is bound to grow.

Goals

To share personal feelings of vulnerability and exposure.
To build trust and intimacy.

Group size

Unlimited.

Time

5–10 minutes.

Materials

Goldfish Bowl worksheets; goldfish bowl (optional).

Process

☞ *Best suited for ongoing groups or longer sessions where participants will be working together on specific problems and issues.*

1. After a brief introduction to the group session or workshop, (including a discussion about confidentiality and other group rules), reassure participants that it is normal to feel vulnerable and exposed when participating in a group, especially in a new group where people do not know each other.

   ● **Participation in groups involves some personal exposure or risk,** especially when you are expected to share personal experiences, problems, or life struggles. Admitting you are not perfect, feel self-conscious, or have some aspect of your life you are struggling with can be scary and uncomfortable. It is normal to feel nervous about sharing your vulnerability.

2. Distribute **Goldfish Bowl** worksheets and encourage everyone to explore areas where they feel exposed. (2–3 minutes)
   ➤ Think about the areas of your life in which you feel exposed and write examples in the goldfish bowl.
      ➤ If possible, include a way you feel exposed by participation in this group.

3. Set an empty goldfish bowl on a chair in the center of the room and ask participants to form a circle with their chairs around the bowl for sharing. (3–4 minutes)
   ☞ *If your group is larger than 10 or 12 people, form several small groups.*
   ➤ Starting with the oldest person in your group, go around the circle and introduce yourself, sharing at a level you are comfortable the ways you feel exposed.
   ➤ After you have introduced yourself and shared vulnerabilities, put your worksheet in the goldfish bowl and allow the next person to share the ways they feel like they too are in a goldfish bowl.
   ➤ Continue to go around the group, allowing each person time to share without interruption.

4. Lead a short discussion about what participants might need from the group to feel less exposed or vulnerable. Incorporate ideas with group ground rules discussed earlier, focusing especially on confidentiality, respect, and acceptance.
   ☞ *If you want to, leave the goldfish bowl sitting out during the entire session as a reminder to participants that everyone has vulnerabilities that need to be honored and respected.*

Variations
   ▪ Work groups might use **Goldfish Bowl** as part of a staff retreat, sharing areas of work where they feel exposed or vulnerable.

■ This is a powerful icebreaker for therapy and support groups, especially those in which people may be feeling a lot of shame about a particular problem, such as alcoholism, eating disorders, or sexual abuse.

GOLDFISH BOWL

31 Disguises

This disarming exercise encourages people to lower their defenses and let others know the real person behind the disguise.

Goals

To increase intimacy.

To build a supportive, accepting group atmosphere.

Group size

Unlimited.

Time

10–15 minutes.

Materials

Disguises worksheets; pair of plastic (gag) glasses with big nose and mustache to be given as a door prize.

Process

Ask everyone to drop their name in a hat before the start of the session for a door-prize drawing at the end of the exercise. For extra hilarity, wear the door prize glasses and mustache during the chalktalk.

1. Introduce this exercise by talking about disguises as normal, human methods of self-protection.

   • **Everyone needs a disguise sometimes:** to present a good front, maintain a certain image, fulfill a role, project your best self, and have some control over what you reveal to others about yourself.

   • **Many things can be used to disguise your true self:** clothes (wearing a power suit when you feel insecure), hairstyles (using long hair to cover your face or eyes), manner of speech (hiding anger behind a soft, sweet voice), social role (forcing yourself to be the life of the party when you are really shy), body posture (shrinking into the woodwork), and other tactics.

2. Hand out **Disguises** worksheets and ask participants to reflect on disguises they use for hiding their true self. (3–4 minutes)
   ➤ Think about things you do to hide your true self.
      ➣ What externals hide the real you: clothes, speech, job, money, body appearance, or political office?
      ➣ What other ways do you disguise your true self: pretending to be perfect, using humor to cover your feelings, or being a loner?
   ➤ Write your favorite disguises on your worksheet, then reflect on what each disguise hides about you.

3. Ask participants to share their disguises with another participant. (4–6 minutes)
   ➤ Pair up with a neighbor whom you do not know well.
   ➤ Decide who will go first, then share your favorite disguises with your partner.
      ➣ Describe each disguise and its purpose for you.
   ➤ After 2 minutes, reverse roles.

4. Reconvene the group, inviting people to share disguise examples, then announce that some lucky person will now win the door prize. Draw a name, then ask the winner to model the gag glasses for the group before continuing your program.

Variations
▦ This process would be suitable for educational, growth, support, and therapy groups. Have people identify disguises for sadness, grief, anger, rage, fear, and insecurity, and discuss them in the group.

DISGUISES

32 Risky Business

Participants explore an important component of mental health: taking risks and living life to its fullest.

Goals

To reflect on the positive and negative consequences of risks taken and not taken.

To raise awareness of personal attitudes about taking risks.

Group size

Unlimited.

Time

5–10 minutes.

Materials

Risky Business worksheets.

Process

1. Set a context for this exercise by making the following chalktalk point about risk-taking.

   ● **Taking risks is a key component of mental health.** The ability to take risks enables us to live life to its fullest, try new things, let go of control, and enjoy the freedom of creativity and personal growth. For example, taking the risk to love someone gives you the opportunity to experience the joys of intimacy and commitment. Taking business risks opens up possibilities of advancing your career and work goals.

2. Distribute the **Risky Business** worksheets, then guide participants through reflection on personal risk taking.

➤ What are three of the most risky things you've tried and the outcomes of those risks?

> Record your three biggest risks in the first section of your worksheet.

➤ What are three times you've backed down from risk and later regretted it?

> List those risks you've avoided and regretted.

➤ What are three times you've backed down from risk and were glad you did?

> Make note of three risks you're glad you avoided.

➤ Now, look over your lists. What are your reactions to what you see?

> In the next space, jot down your reflections, insights, and feelings about your risk lists.

➤ In the final section of your worksheet, describe yourself as a risk taker, using a single sentence (e.g., I'm a high risk taker, I'm a risk avoider, I take risks only when there is a very high chance of success).

3. Conduct a short survey to see how many people in the audience consider themselves to be high risk takers. Reassure everyone in the group that during this session they will not be forced to take more risk than they personally want to take.

Variations

▨ Instead of using worksheets, form small groups, instruct people to sit in a circle, and give each group a pair of dice. Have people toss the dice and ask the person with the lowest score to share first. People then take turns responding to the questions on the worksheet. To save time, omit all questions except the one asking people to describe in one sentence the kind of risk taker they are.

RISKY BUSINESS

 List three of the most risky things you've done and describe the outcomes.

 List three times you've backed down from risk and later regretted it.

 List three times you've backed down from risk and were glad you did.

© 1997 Whole Person Associates 210 W Michigan Duluth MN 55802-1908   800-247-6789

33 Stress Shots

Participants bring props from home to affirm their coping skills as they recall storms they've weathered in the past.

Goals

To remember past successes in managing stress and to affirm coping skills used in dealing with life at that time.

To reflect on the current use of coping skills that were helpful in the past.

Group size

Best for ongoing groups of 6–8 participants.

Time

15–20 minutes.

Materials

Participants need to bring from home three photos, taken at different times of their life, that in some way represent the stress going on at that time.

Process

☞ *This exercise requires participants to do some homework prior to the session, so it is appropriate only for ongoing groups or for groups of people who have regular contact and communication with each other.*

1. Announce the homework assignment by mail, phone, or a previous group meeting.
   ➤ Spend some time looking through your family photo albums, looking for pictures of you at different times of your life.

➤ Pick out three pictures which in some way represent the stress your were experiencing at those three points of your life. You might choose a photo from your son's graduation, the birth of your fourth child, or at the time of your Dad's illness.

➤ Choose any three that are meaningful to you and remind you of the stresses and strains of that period.

➤ Bring these three pictures with you to the group meeting.

2. Start the next session by asking if everyone remembered to bring three pictures of themselves.

☞ *There will probably be a few people who forgot to do their homework. Tell these people they can conjure up mental pictures of themselves at three different times of their life and use these images and memories for sharing.*

3. Instruct participants to sit in a circle facing each other and to share stories about their stress photos.

➤ Take turns showing your three stress photos and telling about the stress going on in your life at the time the picture was taken.

☞ *Provide several relevant examples (e.g., the excitement, joy, grief, and tension going on when your son graduated from high school or the sadness, confusion, and anticipation when you moved to a new home). Better yet, bring your own pictures and use them and your descriptions to model the process.*

➤ Then go back and show your photos a second time. This time talk about the positive and negative coping skills you used to deal with stress going on at the time.

☞ *Again, use your own photos and coping strategies to set the tone or give some examples (e.g., skipping school, walks by the lake, daily readings from a book of meditations, attempts to find humor in the situation, working harder, participation in a support group).*

➤ Each person will have 3 minutes to share your stress shots and your coping skills.

4. When all participants have shared their stress photos, invite the group to discuss the relevance of coping skills they've used in the past. (4 minutes)

➤ Are you still using coping skills you used in the past?

➤ Discuss any changes in your coping skills from the time of your pictures to now. What are the implications or consequences of these changes?

5. Before moving on, ask group members to share insights and discoveries about their ability to cope with stress in the past and the present. End the discussion by affirming the strengths and abilities of all participants to cope with stress.

Variations

▨ This exercise is easily adapted to families by having family groups select pictures from their photo album and use them to affirm the ability of their family to cope with difficult or stressful times.

▨ With large groups in a workshop setting, ask people in advance to bring photos. To create small groups for sharing in Step 3, ask participants to form triads with people who identified at least one stress event different from theirs. For discussions in Step 4, ask triads to pair up as sextets.

▨ Graphic images and photos from magazines or fine art postcards showing people of different ages could be substituted for actual photos.

34 Peaks and Valleys

Participants sketch the highs and lows of their life and reflect on the overall balance of peaks and valleys in their life journey.

Goals

To reflect on joyful and painful times of life and the relative balance of positive and negative experiences.

To create a bond among participants.

Group size

Unlimited.

Time

5–10 minutes.

Materials

Blank paper.

Process

1. Begin by stating that most people have peaks and valleys in their life journey—experiences which stand out as especially joyful and especially painful or difficult. Distribute blank paper and invite participants to reflect on some of their own peaks and valleys. (3–4 minutes)

   ➤ Draw a simple mountain terrain with a high peak and a low valley in it.

   ➤ Near the *peak* of your mountain, write three peak experiences that you consider some of the best times of your life— perhaps falling in love, giving birth to your first child, winning a marathon, taking religious vows, learning a new skill, or traveling abroad.

➤ In the *valley* area, jot down three difficult times of your life—perhaps your parents' divorce, being laid off, the loss of a baby through miscarriage, undergoing chemotherapy, filing for bankruptcy, or being betrayed by someone you trusted.

2. After 4 minutes, interrupt reflections and invite participants to reflect on the overall *balance* of peaks and valleys in their lifetime. (1 minute)

➤ Think about the overall number of peaks and valleys in your lifetime. Is there a balance, or are there more peaks or more valleys?

➤ Somewhere on your paper draw a balance beam with a fulcrum in the middle, showing the relative relationship between peaks and valleys in your life.

➤ If peaks and valleys were at opposite ends of a teeter totter, would it be balanced or tipped in one direction?

3. Invite participants to share personal peaks and valleys with another participant. (2–3 minutes)

➤ Pair up with someone you do not know well.

➤ Take turns sharing the peaks in your life.

➤ Then share the valleys in your life.

➤ If you have time after telling your stories, briefly discuss your reflections about the relative balance (or lack of balance) between peaks and valleys in your life.

4. Ask participants to return to their seats, then invite people to share examples of what they have learned from some of the peaks and valleys in their lives. Use these contributions to emphasize the point that both happy and difficult experiences can build wisdom and strength for coping with future life events.

Variations

▪ This exercise is ideal for spiritual growth groups exploring issues of values and faith. This process is also suitable for therapy and support groups focused on facing problems and coping with adversity.

▪ Work groups could use this exercise as part of a staff retreat or annual review of employee experiences on the job, noting peaks and valleys for individual employees or work teams over a specific period of time.

35 It's for You

An imaginary phone call may bring surprising news for participants about their need to hear a special message from someone.

Goals

To get in touch with internal wisdom.

To explore personal needs for communications and connection.

Group size

Unlimited.

Time

5–10 minutes.

Materials

It's for You worksheets.

Process

1. Invite participants to use the power of their imagination to connect with someone special. (3 minutes)

   ➤ Take a minute and allow yourself to relax.

      ➤ Close your eyes and allow yourself to become quiet as you get in the mood for dreaming.

   ➤ Imagine that phone is ringing—and it's for you!

      ➤ Who would you want to be calling you? It could be anyone you want, near or far, dead or alive, familiar or unknown to you.

      ➤ What you want this person to say to you?

      ➤ Listen for a moment and hear their message for you.

         ☞ *Pause for 15–30 seconds.*

   ➤ And now imagine yourself replying to this person and their message. What do you say as you respond?

---

2. After another minute or so, gently interrupt the reverie and distribute **It's for You** worksheets. Ask participants to record their fantasy phone conversation. (1–2 minutes)

➤ Write down the name of the caller at the top of the sheet.

➤ Record the caller's message in the lines on the telephone.

➤ Add your response to this news below the telephone.

3. When everyone has recorded their messages and responded, invite participants to find a partner and compare notes of their experiences. (4–5 minutes)

➤ Pair up with someone you do not know well and share what feels comfortable about your imaginary phone call.

➤ Each of you has 2 minutes to talk about your phone call.

➤ Be sure to share any discoveries you made about your personal needs for contact, communication, or information from a particular person.

4. Reconvene the group and ask for a few stories, insights, or learnings about the need for contact and communication.

☞ *Some people may express the desire to act on the message they received or contact the caller. Affirm those options, but also encourage people who had a less powerful experience to consider alternative ways they might meet their contact needs.*

Variations

▨ Career-development groups or groups of college students could use this exercise as part of an exploration of job interests: imagining phone calls from prospective employers offering their dream job and describing specific features and job duties they would love.

▨ This is a powerful exercise for grief groups or therapy groups in which people are working on resolving unfinished business with family members or friends who have been lost through death, divorce, or other disconnection.

▨ To add a little punch, start off with an old-fashioned game of Telephone, passing a message about communication around the group or down the rows if large groups are seated auditorium-style.

▨ To help participants focus on their individual needs at the beginning of a group meeting, use this process, but substitute the question, *What do you need to hear during this session?*

© 1997 Whole Person Associates 210 W Michigan Duluth MN 55802-1908   800-247-6789

IT'S FOR YOU

A message from

36 Channel Surfing

Participants use imaginary powers to tune into a chosen year of their life and watch themselves on TV.

Goals

To practice creative visualization as a tool for insight and a catalyst for personal growth.

To enhance self-esteem through the awareness of personal perception and the power of choice.

Group size

Unlimited. Can also be used with individuals.

Time

10–15 minutes.

Materials

Channel Surfing script. Optional: soft instrumental jazz or classical music with CD or cassette player.

Process

☞ *This process assumes that participants have had some experience with or preparation for guided imagery.*

1. Introduce the visualization by announcing that participants will have the opportunity to visit any year of their life—past, present or future—and focus on real or imagined events occurring during that time of their life.

2. Review basic principles of guided imagery.
   ● Close your eyes, take a few deep breaths, and allow your body to relax and your mind to clear.

● Be open to your inner vision. Just allow images to unfold without trying to direct or control them.

● Remember, you are in charge. You can stop the process at any time, simply by opening your eyes.

3. Ask people to get as comfortable as possible, then guide the visualization by reading the **Channel Surfing** script on pages 119 and 120. (5–6 minutes)

☞ *Read slowly enough so that people have time for the images to form. Pause briefly (5 seconds) at the . . . marks. Otherwise follow your own rhythm and the indicated times.*

4. When nearly everyone has opened their eyes, gently encourage folks to return their attention to the present moment. Invite participants to share their experiences with another group member. (4–5 minutes)

➤ Pair up with another person and take turns sharing your experiences in the visualization.

➤ At whatever level feels comfortable, tell each other what you saw when you went channel surfing through the years of your life.

➤ Each person has 2 minutes to share experiences, observations, and feelings while channel surfing.

5. After 4–5 minutes, reconvene the group and ask if anyone wants to share what they learned from their TV experience. If possible, relate this new awareness to the group's learning objectives, emphasizing the importance of self-awareness for growth and change.

Thanks to Richard Boyum, EdD, University of Wisconsin–Eau Claire, for this powerful self-awareness tool. We feel privileged to benefit from the fruits of Richard's enormous gift for creative imagery.

Variations

▨ This is a wonderful exercise for any group exploring developmental issues, such as family of origin experiences, aging issues, or personal identify development.

▨ Channel surfing is easily adapted for specific topics or issues (e.g., eating disorders groups could focus on body image, people in addictions recovery could use it to explore the progression of their illness and recovery, employees could review their job history, wellness programs could explore health or self-care histories).

Channel Surfing Script

Take a deep breath and slowly blow the air out in a big sigh,
letting yourself relax as much as possible. . . .

Gently close your eyes and allow your mind to empty,
letting any thoughts or distractions float easily away
as you allow your inner vision to waken. . . .

Imagine in your mind's eye
that you are sitting in front of a television set . . .
with a rather large screen. . . .

Notice the power switch which is easy to reach. . . .
Be aware that you have control. . . .
Anytime you wish you may turn the set on or off . . .
Or turn the volume up or down. . . .
So you are in charge of how intensely you become involved
in whatever you choose to watch. . . .

Also notice the channel indicator
with its large display numbers. . . .
This special indicator includes numbers to represent
every year of your life . . .

from the time of your birth at 0 . . .
to your present age . . . and on into the future. . . .
Now notice the fine tuning knob. . . .
This handy little dial allows you to tune in
to actual months, weeks, or days
during any given year of your life. . . .
Take another deep breath. . . .
And as you breathe out,
reach over and turn on the television. . . .
The channel indicator is automatically set at 30. . . .
Begin counting up or down
as you slowly turn the channel indicator
until you find a year you would like to watch. . . .

☞ Pause 15 seconds.

When you have found a year that appeals to you,
settle back and watch the show. . . .
Observe whatever images and sounds come to you
from that year of your life. . . .
Continue to watch and observe as long as you want. . . .

☞ Pause 1 minute or more.

At a moment of your choosing . . .
turn the channel indicator back to your present age . . .
and then reach over and turn off the television.

As the screen darkens in your mind . . .
slowly open your eyes
and return your attention to the present.

© 1997 Whole Person Associates 210 W Michigan Duluth MN 55802-1908   800-247-6789

37 Comfort Zone

Participants explore their need for comfort on several levels—physical, emotional, spiritual, and interpersonal—and prescribe their own relief measures.

Goals

To identify needs for physical, emotional, spiritual, and interpersonal comfort and explore potential sources of comfort.

To ease initial discomfort in the group setting.

Group size

Unlimited. Can also be used with individuals.

Time

5–10 minutes.

Materials

Comfort Zone worksheets.

Process

☞ *This process is especially appropriate for people recovering from trauma, grief and loss, illness and injury, relationship hurts, depression, burnout, or stress.*

1. Set the context for this exercise by relating the need for comfort to specific issues of your audience.
   - Given all the stresses and strains of everyday life and work, most people need comfort every day. However, most of us are not very imaginative or proficient at giving ourselves the comfort we truly need.
   - At the beginning of any experience like this one, everyone's comfort zone is stretched. Once we get to know one another a bit, everyone will feel more comfortable.

2. Distribute **Comfort Zone** worksheets and invite participants to explore current comfort needs from a whole person perspective. (5 minutes)

> Close your eyes and tune in to your body, mind, and spirit. Consider in what ways you need comfort today.

> Are you in need of *physical* comfort?

>> Perhaps you're cold or hungry or tired. Maybe you have some aches or pains or just feel antsy and uncomfortable in your chair. Perhaps you yearn for a soothing massage, a stretch break, a workout, or a warm drink.

>> Tune in to your physical comfort needs and jot down those you identify in the box at the top left of your worksheet.

> What about *emotional* comfort needs?

>> Are you feeling discouraged or angry or resentful? Are you worried or concerned? Do you need to calm the butterflies or turn down the pressure? Perhaps you need someone to reassure you that your actions are appropriate or give you support for the difficulties you are facing.

>> Pay attention to your needs for emotional comfort and record them on the left of your worksheet.

> Are you aware of any *interpersonal* comfort needs?

>> Perhaps you're feeling lonely or out of touch. Maybe you're yearning for stimulation and recharging. Or needing affirmation that you are loved or respected. Are you hoping for the relief of relaxing with family or friends? Or the fun of playing a game or the comfort of an intimate rendezvous.

>> Write your needs for interpersonal comfort in the appropriate box.

> Are you aware of needing *spiritual* comfort at all?

>> Perhaps you are feeling empty or cynical and doubting. Maybe you're needing comfort from some deep grief or

renewed purpose and meaning in life. Maybe you need forgiveness for some actions you regret—or need to forgive someone else. Perhaps your soul yearns for prayer, meditation, or worship.

> Whatever you can discern about your need for spiritual comfort, write some notes in the box on your worksheet.

3. Once their needs are identified, invite participants to reflect on exactly what would comfort them. (3 minutes)

> Now go back and look at the comfort needs you identified in each area and ask yourself exactly what would comfort you on this level of your being.

> In the right column of your worksheet, write specific, practical, realistic ideas of what would comfort you physically, emotionally, interpersonally, and spiritually.

> Try to personalize your ideas or plans and identify what will work for you.

> Do not judge or criticize yourself for your comfort needs and plans, even if they seem silly or trivial to you.

4. Invite participants to share comfort needs with another participant. (4–5 minutes)

> Pair up with someone and tell that person whatever you wish about your comfort needs and the ways you could get those needs fulfilled.

> Take turns talking and listening to each other.

> You have 5 minutes total.

5. After 4–5 minutes, reconvene the group and solicit specific comfort ideas for each of the four dimensions.

6. End the discussion by encouraging participants to seek the comfort they need when they leave the group session or, if appropriate, during the session if this is part of the group's purpose or contract.

Variations

> ▪ In family groups with older children, each family member could fill out a worksheet, share needs for comfort with each other, then discuss possibilities of offering each other needed comfort.

> ▪ This is an ideal exercise for church support groups, grief groups, and retreats as people explore needs for healing from losses and disappointments.

© 1997 Whole Person Associates 210 W Michigan Duluth MN 55802-1908   800-247-6789

COMFORT ZONE

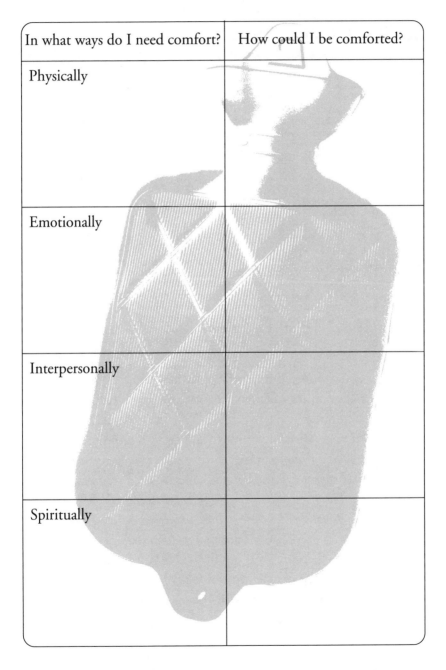

In what ways do I need comfort?	How could I be comforted?
Physically	
Emotionally	
Interpersonally	
Spiritually	

38 Stamps of Approval

This simple exercise reminds participants that they always have the power to give themselves the approval they want and need.

Goals

To identify personal needs for approval.

To practice self-approval.

Group size

Unlimited.

Time

5–10 minutes.

Materials

Stamp of Approval worksheets.

Process

1. Give everyone a **Stamp of Approval** worksheet. Invite people to reflect on areas of their life where they are needing approval. (3–4 minutes)

   ➤ In what areas of your life do you need approval?

      ☞ *Give lots of examples (e.g., career choice, work achievements, family relationships, parenting decisions, community activities, friendship patterns, health goals, creative pursuits, problem-solving, body appearance, job performance, charm, leadership potential).*

   ➤ Are there areas of your life where you feel uncertain, lack self-confidence, or need reassurance?

   ➤ Are there areas where you feel your efforts have gone unrecognized or unappreciated by others?

➤ On the left side of your worksheet, write some specific examples of areas in which you want or need approval.

2. Remind people that approval is a gift they have the power to give themselves anytime they want or need it. Invite participants to practice giving themselves a stamp of approval today. (3–4 minutes)

➤ Start with the first example you wrote and give yourself the stamp of approval that you need.

➤ On the lines to the right of the stamp, write exactly what you need to tell yourself to gain approval about that situation or issue.

➤ Use "I" statements, stated in positive words or statements which you can accept and believe.

☞ *Give lots of examples (e.g., I approve of my career choices; I affirm my work achievements; I accept my decision to work part-time to balance work and family; I believe I am a good parent).*

3. If time allows, ask people to turn to a neighbor whom they do not know well and share one or more personal stamps of approval.

Variations

▨ In work settings, build team support by passing around worksheets and asking each person to give coworkers stamps of approval for contributions to job productivity.

▨ For playful variations, experiment with using actual ink pads and funny stamps of approval that participants can stamp on worksheets or on the hands of other group members.

Combine this process with **Personal Affirmation**, page 165. Ask participants to join together in *whispering*, then *speaking*, and finally *shouting* their individual approval messages in chorus.

I need _____

I need _____

I need _____

I need _____

I need _____

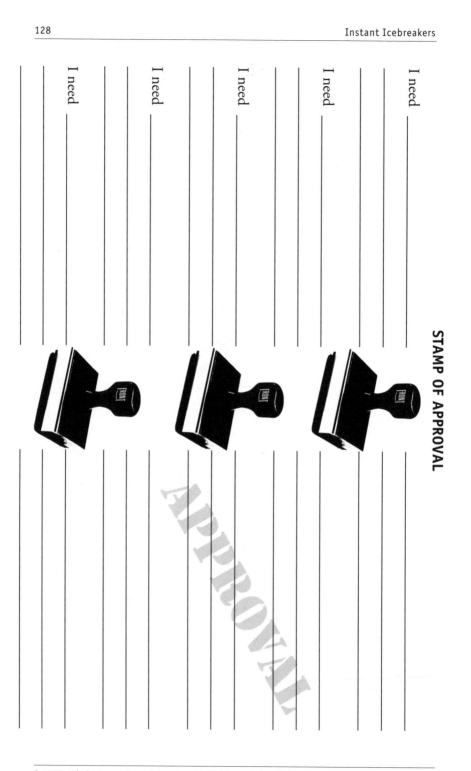

STAMP OF APPROVAL

39 Crystal Ball

In this empowering icebreaker or closing ritual, participants receive a crystal ball to help them make decisions about important issues.

Goals

To rely on inner wisdom and intuition for important insights and decisions.

To promote trust, patience, and acceptance of self during times of uncertainty.

Group size

Unlimited.

Time

5–10 minutes.

Materials

Small crystal marbles for all participants.

Process

1. Distribute marbles to all participants. Announce that these marbles are actually miniature crystal balls. (1 minute)

   ➤ This crystal ball can help you make important decisions or resolve difficult life issues.

      ➤ When you look into your crystal ball, answers to certain questions may come very clearly; in other cases, they may remain unclear. In either case, the ball will give you access to insights about yourself.

      ➤ You can carry this crystal ball with you and use it whenever you want or need it.

© 1997 Whole Person Associates 210 W Michigan Duluth MN 55802-1908   800-247-6789

2. Invite participants to take a moment to experiment with their crystal balls. (1 minute)

> First, think of a life situation, problem, dilemma, or decision you are facing and for which you need inspiration.

☞ *Pause while people get focused.*

> Now, look into your crystal ball and focus on that concern.

> Sit quietly and gaze into your crystal ball, reflecting on your dilemma and waiting for insights.

> When you are ready, put your crystal ball away.

3. After 2–3 minutes, invite participants to share examples of insights and discoveries they made when looking into their crystal balls. Congratulate volunteers for trusting their inner wisdom.

4. In closing, remind participants that achieving clarity and resolving issues takes time.

● **It is important to be patient and accepting of yourself.** Sometimes you will experience confusion and uncertainty, and your ball may be cloudy. Trust that insights and answers will eventually come to you because you have kept the door to your inner self open.

Variation

■ The crystal ball idea works well for therapy groups, growth groups, or work groups seeking solutions to problems or envisioning future growth and development; family groups dealing with everyday stress and relationship conflicts; other groups or individuals wanting to access personal creativity and intuition.

This metaphorical exercise was inspired by Richard Boyum, EdD, University of Wisconsin–Eau Claire, who is a veritable roman candle of creative ideas for working with individuals or groups.

Change Agents

The dozen icebreakers in this section are designed to create a climate for change through reflection, analysis, goal-setting, problem-solving, and clarification of relevant life issues in the context of group support.

40 Self-Care Stopwatch

This exercise is especially relevant for participants trying to *stop* addictive behaviors and *watch* themselves so that they don't slip back into old, negative habits.

Goals

To identify unhealthy behavior habits or patterns which need to be stopped.

To raise awareness of the risks of slipping into old, self-destructive behaviors.

Group size

Unlimited. Can also be used with individuals.

Time

10–15 minutes.

Materials

Self-Care Stopwatch worksheets.

Process

☞ *This process is an ideal follow-up to a presentation on addictions such as eating, gambling, drinking or using other drugs, smoking, shopping, spending money, working, exercising, or relationships.*

1. Introduce the exercise with a brief chalktalk appropriate to your group and specific learning objectives.
   ● **All of us have at least a few bad habits** or negative behavior patterns that may threaten our health, interfere with our relationships, or diminish our satisfaction with life.

2. Distribute **Self-Care Stopwatch** worksheets and challenge participants to take an honest look at their own addictive behaviors or self-destructive patterns. (3 minutes)

➤ Take a moment to consider the extent to which you rely on addictive behavior to cope with stress? What habits or patterns do you have that you think are unhealthy or self-destructive?

> Do you use food, alcohol, other drugs (including caffeine), money, shopping, work, gambling, smoking, or relationships as a way to soothe your feelings or distract yourself from problems?

> Is your relationship with any of these addictive substances becoming destructive or causing you (or your family, friends, and work colleagues) problems or concern?

➤ On your worksheet, write down some of the behaviors or patterns you need to *stop*.

☞ *Give several examples your participants will identify with (e.g., I need to stop working sixteen hours a day to avoid my loneliness since my divorce; I need to stop pigging out on junk food when I am angry at my boyfriend; I need to stop buying things every time I am depressed or bored).*

➤ Write down the behaviors or patterns you need to *watch* on the second line.

☞ *Again, give appropriate examples (e.g., I need to watch my tendency to overeat; I need to watch my habit of drinking after work; I need to watch my smoking when I'm stressed or tense; I need to watch my pattern of hopping from relationship to relationship too quickly).*

3. Ask participants to form groups of 6–8 people based on their favorite beverage (or junk food).

☞ *Divide the total number of participants by 7. This is the number of groups you will need. Choose a common beverage (or junk food) for each group and designate an area of the room for lovers of that brand to gather. Adjust the groups, if necessary, so none is larger than 8 people or smaller than 6.*

4. As soon as groups are settled, give instructions for sharing self-care plans. (5 minutes)

> Introduce yourself to the group and share as much as you wish about your hopes and plans for self-care.

>> What would you like to *stop* doing?

>> Where are you going to *watch* yourself in the future?

5. Reconvene the whole group and ask for examples from the small groups. Use these self-care issues to set your agenda for the session.

6. At the end of the session, or when it fits best with your teaching design, summarize the *stop* and *watch* aspects of self care.

● **Self-care usually involves** *stopping* **and** *watching* **yourself.** It means you *stop* doing things to hurt yourself and start *watching* over yourself to make sure that you don't become careless or destructive. Approach this process with a firm, but loving attitude toward yourself, treating yourself as you would your best friend or a dear family member.

Variations

▦ Health education and fitness groups can use the **Self-Care Stopwatch** to identify habits which are negatively affecting physical health, such as eating a high fat diet or living a sedentary life style. For a more holistic perspective, create a self-care stopwatch for each dimension of well-being: physical, emotional, mental, relationships, spiritual, lifestyle, work, etc.

▦ Educational, support, or therapy groups can adapt this exercise to relationship issues or patterns, such as *stopping* conflict avoidance and *watching* self for dishonesty or lack of assertiveness in relationships.

▦ For groups focused on changing negative patterns in the workplace, use the stopwatch as a closing/planning tool to identify on-the-job behaviors to *stop* and *watch*.

SELF-CARE STOPWATCH

I need to STOP

I need to WATCH

41 Behind the Eight-Ball

This intriguing exercise helps participants quickly identify troublesome life situations and offers hope for getting out of tight spots.

Goals

To identify personal stressors or life dilemmas affecting mental or physical health.

To reframe stress, crisis, and conflict as an opportunity for change.

Group size

Unlimited. Can also be used with individuals.

Time

10–15 minutes.

Materials

Behind the Eight-Ball worksheets; newsprint; marker.

Process

☞*Adjust levels of sharing according to the nature of your audience and purpose of the group. For work groups, eliminate sharing about personal life dilemmas and focus only on ways people are behind the eight-ball at work.*

1. Ask participants if they are familiar with the concept of *being behind the eight-ball.* Solicit a few definitions and examples from the group, summarizing with an observation and a challenge.

   ● **Being behind the eight-ball means you're in a tight spot.**
      Whether the game is pool or the game of life, getting out

from behind the eight-ball requires creative maneuvering, skill, and willingness to take risks. It is difficult, but possible.

2. Hand out **Behind the Eight-Ball** worksheets, and invite participants to reflect on ways they are behind the eight-ball in their personal or work life. (3–4 minutes)

➤ In what ways are you behind the eight-ball in your personal or work life?

➢ What challenges, stresses, conflicts, or life dilemmas are you facing?

☞ *Prime the pump with lots of examples relevant to your audience (e.g., Are you anticipating layoffs, facing a huge debt with limited financial resources, being asked to either quit drinking or lose your girlfriend, aware that if you don't stop smoking you are a high risk for heart attack, trying to meet a deadline at work?).*

➢ What situations are you in that are restricting your choices and perhaps threatening your mental or physical health?

☞ *Again, give plenty of provocative examples (e.g., Have you been arrested for driving under the influence of alcohol and ordered to attend alcohol education classes, been placed on probation at work, caught in an abusive relationship that is making you feel crazy, or said some things you didn't mean, causing your best friend to stop speaking to you?).*

➤ On your worksheet, list some of the ways you are behind the eight-ball in your life these days.

3. Invite participants to form small groups based on birth dates.

➤ Find 3 other people who share your birth date numeral second digit (e.g., 5th and 15th, or 10th, 20th, and 30th).

☞ *Adjust these instructions for the size of your group. These instructions should work well for groups of 40–50. With small groups, use single digits, teens, and twenties/thirties birth dates. Be sure to help loners and extras find a group.*

4. As soon as quartets are settled, give instructions for discussion. (8 minutes)

> ➤ Take turns introducing yourselves and sharing some of the ways you are behind the eight-ball these days.

> ➤ Each person has 2 minutes to share.

> ☞ *Remind participants that whatever is shared is to be kept strictly confidential and not discussed outside the group.*

5. Reconvene the entire group and shift the focus to solution finding. Ask people to share strategies they've used successfully in the past to get out from behind the eight-ball. Paraphrase and summarize each strategy as it is described. List all suggested strategies on newsprint and use them as an invitation to your next teaching module.

> ● **Being in a tight dilemma is an opportunity** for change and for personal and professional growth. That's what we're here for!

Variations

> ▣ This exercise is perfect for groups of people facing the negative consequences of personal behavior, such as gambling, alcohol or drug treatment groups, debt management and consumer credit counseling groups, batterers' anger control groups, and prisoner education or counseling groups.

> ▣ On a lighter note, this exercise is also appropriate for groups working on issues such as stress management, career development, health education and wellness, values clarification, relationships, and life planning.

> ▣ This exercise can also be used with families. Ask each family member to fill out a **Behind the Eight-Ball** worksheet and share it with each other.

BEHIND THE EIGHT-BALL

42 Turning Points

In this thoughtful exercise, participants explore how their self-image has been shaped by significant turning points in life.

Goals

To explore ways in which significant turning points have shaped self-image.

To raise self-awareness and promote learning from life changes.

Group size

Unlimited.

Time

10–15 minutes.

Materials

Blank paper.

Process

1. Introduce the exercise with a few comments on the impact of life events on self-concept. Illustrate your observations with examples relevant to your audience, setting, and educational goals.

   ● **Life changes affect your self-image.** Some turning points, such as graduation from college or getting a promotion, can enhance self-image and make you feel better about yourself. Other changes, such as unemployment or loss of income, can cause you to feel diminished as a person.

2. Distribute blank paper and guide participants in an exploration of a significant turning point in their life and its effect on them. (4–5 minutes)

➤ Think back to some turning point in your life such as graduation, marriage, divorce, new job, or the birth of children.

➤ When you have a specific incident in mind, write it at the
top of your paper and write a few sentences that describe
your turning point in more detail.

☞ *Pause until everyone has identified a turning point and
written about it.*

➤ Was this a positive or negative experience for you?

➤ What positive and negative effects did this experience
have on you? Record your observations.

☞ *Pause a minute or so here and after the next questions
so people have time to think and write.*

➤ How did the turning point help you grow as a person?

➤ List a few of the ways this experience made you a better
or wiser person.

➤ Now consider in what ways this turning point has influenced your overall self-image.

➤ Make some notes about the impact of this experience on
your sense of self.

3. Give instructions for forming small groups.

➤ Find 2 or 3 people whom you do not know well. Try to
choose people with different turning points.

➤ When you have a group of 3 or 4, sit down together in a
circle and introduce yourselves.

4. When groups are settled and introductions made, invite participants to share their turning point discoveries.

➤ Take turns sharing your turning point experiences and how
they influenced your self-image. Don't forget to talk about
how your turning point helped you grow.

➤ Take 1 or 2 minutes each.

➤ The oldest person should start.

5. Reconvene the group and ask volunteers to share examples of

how turning points helped them to grow or to see themselves more positively. Summarize comments and acknowledge that this workshop might be a turning point for some individuals.

Variations

- At the closing session of a therapy or growth group, use this process for identifying turning points in the life of the group and their impact on individual group members.

43 Life is Too Short

In this short, reflective exercise, participants quickly identify values and priorities and consider what is truly important to them.

Goals

To clarify values and goals.

To identify personal time wasters and dreams that have been postponed.

Group size

Unlimited.

Time

5–10 minutes.

Materials

Blank paper.

Process

1. Introduce the icebreaker with a few comments on the precious nature of each moment of life—and the observation that life is too short . . . to waste.

2. Announce that the next few minutes offer an opportunity for participants to consider what is truly important to them and gain some insight on how they want to spend the remaining moments of their lives.

3. Distribute blank paper and guide people through the reflection process. (2 minutes)

   ➤ Fold your paper in half vertically, so there are two columns.
      ➤ Label the left column **Life is too short to . . .** and label the right column **Life is too short** *not* **to . . .**

➤ In the left-hand **Life is too short to** . . . column, list several activities that aren't worth spending your time at.

☞ *Spark people's thinking with lots of examples (e.g., life is too short to iron permapress clothes, wait until a relationship develops, watch commercials, finish everything, redial, shop at rush hour, make bread from scratch, dust the knickknacks, read all the junk mail, listen to telemarketers, work overtime, change your own oil).*

➤ Jot down as many potential life and time wasters you can think of.

4. After 2 minutes, interrupt reflections and invite participants to focus on goals, dreams, and pleasures which may have been neglected or postponed. (2 minutes)

➤ In the right-hand **Life is too short *not* to** . . . column, write several dreams or goals you yearn to fulfill, experiences you'd enjoy, but rarely find time for.

☞ *Again, give lots of examples (e.g., life is too short **not** to listen to fine music, write a love note, play hooky on a beautiful day, take a class in French, try brussels sprouts, explore Alaska, stay in touch with family, host an exchange student or foreign instructor, take a vacation, learn how to fly, snuggle with a pet, meet your neighbors).*

➤ Jot down as many joyful life enhancers you can think of.

5. After 2 minutes, interrupt and solicit examples of life wasters and life enhancers.

6. In closing, encourage everyone to eliminate some of their time wasters and invest time and energy on something more important to them. (1 minute)

➤ Look over your **Life is too short to** . . . list again and underline one or two activities that you consider time and life wasters that you definitely want to stop doing.

➤ Review your **Life is too short *not* to** . . . list and underline

© 1997 Whole Person Associates 210 W Michigan Duluth MN 55802-1908   800-247-6789

one or two life enhancers that you definitely want to pursue in the next few days or months.

7. If possible, incorporate **Life is too short to . . .** ideas into the rest of the workshop or group session, reminding people that they can choose to spend time on things most important to them, while letting go of life wasters.

Variations

▨ After Steps 4 and 6, have participants compare notes on life wasters and life enhancers in pairs or small groups.

▨ This is a great addition to workshops focused on behavior change, stress management, and values clarification. Work groups could use this exercise as a planning tool for discussion about work priorities, values, and goals.

44 Random Reasons

When participants' reasons for making behavior changes are scrambled with other people's reasons, the result is hilarious.

Goals

To encourage a lighthearted, humorous attitude toward change. To have fun and get energized.

Group size

Unlimited.

Time

5–10 minutes.

Materials

Blank 3"x5" cards (2 per participant).

Process

☞ *After participants have spent some time taking a serious look at health concerns or problems and have identified goals and reasons for change, introduce this process as part of an attempt to change the mood of the group.*

1. Acknowledge that while making behavior changes can be serious business, it's a good idea to keep problems in perspective and not take ourselves too seriously.

2. Introduce the exercise as a playful attempt to keep a lighthearted approach to change. Ask participants to play along and see what happens when their goals and reasons for change are mixed up and randomly rematched with those of other participants.

    ☞ *Strive for a respectful but playful mood. Take care that*

participants understand that this is just a humorous diver-
sion and do not think or feel that you are making fun of them.

3. Give each participants two 3"x5" cards and guide them through the goal-setting and scrambling process. (1–2 minutes)

   ➤ On one card, write an unhealthy behavior pattern that you would like to give up or change. Phrase it in this way: *I want to (stop/quit/give up) . . . (undesirable behavior).*

      ☞ *Give appropriate examples (e.g., stop drinking coffee all day at work; give up soap operas, quit smoking).*

   ➤ On the other card, write your reasons for wanting to make this change. Phrase it to complete the sentence you wrote on your first card: . . . *so I won't (undesirable outcome); . . . so I will/can (desirable outcome).*

      ☞ *Give examples of card pairs (e.g. I want to quit drinking coffee all day . . . so I won't be so nervous and irritable when I come home from work; I want to give up soap operas . . . so I can get my studying done; I want to stop smoking . . . so I don't get cancer).*

4. When everyone has completed their *give up* card and *reason* card, collect all the *give up* cards, shuffle them thoroughly, and put them in one pile. Then collect all the *reasons* cards, shuffle them, and put them in a separate pile.

5. Randomly draw one *give up* card and one *reason* card and read them aloud to the group. Continue drawing *give up* and *reason* cards, reading them aloud, and enjoying the hilarity of the juxtapositions.

6. Close by acknowledging that this has been a time for laughter and relief from the serious business of change. But remind people of the surprisingly helpful combinations that emerged in the process.

45 1–2–3 Change!

This simple process brings to light interesting reflections on change.

Goals

To reflect on personal life changes.

To explore the difference between voluntary change and change over which you have no control.

Group size

Unlimited.

Time

10–15 minutes.

Materials

1–2–3 Change worksheets. Optional: recording of Judy Collins' "Everything Changes," (from her *Bread and Roses* album), cassette or CD player.

Process

☞ *Try playing a portion or all of Judy Collins' song, "Everything Changes," as a prelude to this reflection. Encourage participants to contemplate the change process while listening to the music.*

1. Introduce the icebreaker with a few comments about change and the change process, tailored to your topic and setting.

2. Hand out 1–2–3 Change worksheets. Guide participants through a reflection about change in their life. (4–5 minutes)

   ➤ What are some things in your life which you chose to change? Did you choose to move away from home, go to college out of state, become a teacher, live in the country, buy a horse, give up high-fat foods, or end a relationship with an undependable friend?

> Write three things you *chose* to change in the three boxes of the **Chosen** column of your worksheet.

> Now think about the kinds of changes you have experienced where you had *no choice*—changes that were beyond your control. Did you experience the death of a parent, moving to a new city or school, being a person of color in a predominately white workplace, a friend's betrayal, or your daughter's decision to be a single parent?

> Write three things that changed in your life and were beyond your control in the **No Choice** column.

> What kinds of things do you *want to change* about yourself? Would you like to change your sedentary lifestyle, shyness in meeting people, tendency to be critical of others, maxing out your charge card, using procrastination to avoid stress, or not taking enough time with family?

> Write three things you *want to change* about yourself in the **Me** column.

3. Invite participants to get together in small groups and give guidelines for discussion. (5–6 minutes)

> Find 3 other people you do not know well, sit down together, and introduce yourselves.

> Take turns telling each other what life changes have been the hardest for you or caused you the most stress.

> Each person has 2 minutes to share.

4. After 4–5 minutes, reconvene the group and conduct a survey by a show of hands to see which kind of change people thought was the most stressful—change that is chosen or unchosen. Summarize results and lead a short discussion about what it is that makes change more or less stressful.

Thanks to the Rev. Linda Loving, St. Paul, Minnesota, who bailed us out before a workshop once by suggesting this process via long distance.

1–2–3 CHANGE!

CHOSEN		NO CHOICE		ME	
1		1		1	
2		2		2	
3		3		3	

46 Goal Ladder

Participants outline clear, concrete steps toward goals for change, along with supports needed along the way.

Goals

To identify specific behavioral steps and supports needed for reaching goals.

To simplify planning for change.

Group size

Unlimited. Can also be used with individuals.

Time

5–10 minutes.

Materials

Goal Ladder worksheets.

Process

☞ *Use this short planning process in any session focused on problem solving or behavioral change.*

1. After participants have identified goals for change, hand out **Goal Ladder** worksheets, and instruct participants to think about specific steps toward their goal and the type of support they will need along the way. (3 minutes)

   ➤ At the top of the ladder, write your goal as an "I will" statement.

      ☞ *Give several examples that fit your group (e.g., I will go back to college and finish my degree; I will finish my paperwork by noon each Friday; I will improve my relationship with my brother; I will develop a more participatory management style).*

➤ Now consider what steps would be necessary to reach that goal.

    ➤ On the left side of the ladder, below the word steps, list several steps you have *already taken* to help you reach your goal.

    ➤ On the rungs of the ladder, write specific steps you will *need to take* in the future to reach your goal.

        ☞ *Give concrete examples (e.g., I will save money for college tuition, talk to my boss or supervisor about working part-time while going to school, make a new budget based on reduced income).*

➤ Now consider the supports you have and will need in the future if you want to reach your goal.

    ➤ Below the right side of the ladder, list some of the supports your *already have* in striving to reach your goal.

    ➤ On the ladder rungs, write the supports you will *need in the future* if you hope to achieve your goal.

        ☞ *Give relevant examples (e.g., I'll need my spouse's willingness to be primary breadwinner for the next year and my boss's support for working flexible hours).*

2. Ask participants to pair up with a neighbor and share goal ladders. (2–3 minutes)

    ➤ Take turns sharing your goal ladders and describing steps and supports needed to reach your goal, as well as those you already have in place.

    ➤ If talking about your goal ladder triggers ideas about additional steps and supports, take the time to add them now.

Variations

▨ This generic process adapts to almost any type of group or setting, as long as people are working on some form of goal or behavior change.

GOAL LADDER

SUPPORTS

STEPS

47 Ready-Set-Go

Participants evaluate personal readiness for change in this quick and easy assessment.

Goals

To assess personal readiness for the learning experience.

To appreciate attitude, motivation, and humor as variables affecting learning and the ability to change.

Group size

Unlimited.

Time

10–12 minutes.

Materials

Blank paper.

Process

1. At the beginning of the session, invite participants to take a look at their readiness to learn. Distribute blank paper and guide people through a quick, subjective assessment.

    ● Effective learning—and effective behavior change—depends on three key ingredients: **attitude**, **motivation**, and **humor**. You can determine whether you're ready to learn in this session by asking yourself a few simple questions.

    ➤ Fold your paper in half and then open it up again. On the left side write down the three variables: **A** for **Attitude**, **M** for **Motivation**, and **H** for **Humor**.

    ➤ Use these three variables to rate your readiness for learning. Using a scale from 1–10, with 1 representing little or no presence of this ingredient for learning, and 10 indicating a very high presence of this learning ingredient.

☞ *Guide folks through reflection about each change readiness variable.*

➢ Start with **A** for **Attitude.** What is your attitude regarding this learning experience?

➢ Are you positive and optimistic about what might happen, or are you pessimistic or negative before you start?

➢ Rate your *attitude* about being here today, using the 1–10 scale and picking the number that best represents the degree to which you have a positive attitude toward learning today. Write the number down.

➢ Next is **M** for **Motivation.** What is the level of your motivation for learning today?

➢ Are you highly motivated and willing to put time and energy toward learning about this subject with this group, or are you unwilling to invest much effort at this time?

➢ Write a number representing your *motivation.*

➢ Last, but not least, **H** is for **Humor.** Do you have a sense of humor about learning in this environment?

➢ Can you laugh at yourself, remain lighthearted, and roll with the punches, or are you very grim and judgmental in your approach?

➢ Write your *humor* score on your paper.

2. Instruct participants to total their scores for all three dimensions, then explain how to interpret them.

➢ Add your scores for all three change variables.

➢ You are most likely to succeed at learning something valuable today if your score is at least 18.

☞ *Ask for a show of hands to indicate how many folks reached the magic number. Congratulate those who eager and ready to learn. Encourage those whose scores are in the mid-range to consider how they might raise one or more of their scores. Give permission for those with very low scores to consider bailing out right now so they don't waste their time—or else take some quick action to turn up their attitude, turn on their motivation, or tune up their funny bone.*

3. At the end of the session, when participants have identified some specific goals for behavior change, use this assessment again. Repeat Steps 2 and 3, this time asking participants to apply the three criteria to one of their desired behavior changes.

4. Invite participants to share their assessments with partners and then solicit ideas of what people can do if their score is less than 18. Supplement the group's suggestions as needed to provide a quick summary of options.

   ● If necessary, modify the goal to make it more interesting and appealing.

   ● Make a conscious decision to cultivate a positive attitude and a sense of humor.

   ● Spend time with positive people, people who are supportive and encouraging and can make you laugh or take yourself less seriously.

   ● Find new motivations for making this change. Write them down and read them often.

   ● If nothing else works, it may be appropriate to let go of this goal and decide to not change your behavior at this time.

5. Close with a peptalk encouraging participants to use this handy feedback tool whenever they are contemplating change or finding themselves resisting a new experience.

48 Not So Fast

This lighthearted but potent exercise makes people aware of resistance to change and strengthens their resolve to change.

Goals

To become aware of personal and interpersonal resistance to change.

To solidify and affirm decisions to change.

Group size

Unlimited.

Time

15–20 minutes.

Process

☞ *This exercise assumes participants have already identified behavior changes they would like to make.*

1. Begin with a brief chalktalk on the concept of resistance to change. Include references to the specific course content and draw on issues and examples that have surfaced in the group.

   ● **There are always forces resisting change.** When you decide to change something, you are often confronted with your own resistance, combined with subtle and not so subtle pressure from family, friends, neighbors, and coworkers to keep things the same.

   ● We are surrounded by attitudes that get in the way of change. Listen to the chorus: *Don't upset the apple cart; We've always done it this way; Change is too upsetting; What's wrong with the way you are?* These are some of the messages you're likely to hear—sometimes from your own mouth or inner voice—when you try to change.

2. Invite participants to explore this resistance in a simulation game. (8–10 minutes)

> Return to your team and find a place to sit down together.

☞ *If people do not have a team or established small group, create groups of 6–8 people by number of times participants have moved in their life.*

> Take turns assuming the role of **change advocate**, telling the group what you have decided to change in your life.

> When you are a **change advocate,** use a firm, confident voice to describe your goal for change.

> Other group members will take on the role of **devil's advocate**.

> Take turns offering resistance to this change by saying *Not so fast . . .* and giving a reason why the change advocate shouldn't make the stated change.

> As soon as the change advocate states their goal, each **devil's advocate** in turn should say the magic phrase *Not so fast . . .* and give a different, realistic reason why the change advocate should not change.

> When you are a **change advocate,** remain silent and listen to everyone's argument against change without responding or arguing back.

> The person who has the most *Rs* (for resistance) in their name should assume the change advocate role first. Then go around the group counterclockwise.

> Take 1 minute each to state your goal for change and hear the resistance feedback.

☞ *Monitor the process, coaching the groups as needed to keep them on track.*

3. After 3–5 minutes, when the first round of resistance is finished, give instructions for another round.

> Now do a second round, this time with **change advocates** countering resistance they receive from devil's advocates.

> **Change advocates,** this time stand up for yourself. Give a different positive reason for making your desired change in response to each challenge you receive.

> **Devil's advocates** can either repeat their original objection or make up a new one for the second go-around.

> Take turns assuming the role of change advocate and devil's advocate until everyone has a turn to defend their resolution for change.

4. Reconvene the large group and ask people what they learned about resistance. Highlight important insights, then wrap up with a few suggestions for dealing with resistance to change.

   ● **Expect resistance and have a plan for dealing with it.** Resistance is less likely to defeat you if you anticipate it and are prepared to handle it.

   ● **Specific strategies work best.** Arrange to run with a friend so you are not tempted to stay in bed on cold mornings. Research a subject well before you propose a change in policy at work. Anticipate arguments from a spouse about your desire to go to night school and think of possible solutions for problems created by your absence from home.

   ● **Get to know your own internal patterns of resistance** so you can nip them in the bud.

Variations

▦ In work settings, focus on changes in the workplace, with team members taking on the role of resistant employees.

▦ Family groups could have team members assume designated family roles and offer resistance against change goals of one family member.

Thanks to our colleague, Pat Miller, Duluth, Minnesota, for teaching us this powerful technique in a conflict management workshop.

© 1997 Whole Person Associates 210 W Michigan Duluth MN 55802-1908   800-247-6789

49 Strategy Shuffle

This heartening exchange of strategies offers participants fresh perspectives on old problems.

Goals

To break out of a rut and see problems from a new perspective.

To share coping resources with other participants and learn new strategies for dealing with problems.

Group size

Unlimited.

Time

5–10 minutes.

Materials

Strategy Shuffle worksheets; masking tape.

Process

☞ *This process is excellent for groups focused on change, problem-solving, and coping skills.*

1. Ask if people are interested in hearing fresh ideas for coping with old problems. When folks respond affirmatively, hand out **Strategy Shuffle** worksheets and give instructions.

   ➤ Do not write your name on your worksheet; you will be able to recognize your own writing or problem situation when you retrieve your worksheet later.

   ➤ In the first box labeled **My situation**, write a brief description of a problem or challenging situation you have been coping with over the past few months.

➤ In the box labeled **My strategy**, describe the ways you have already tried to cope with the situation.

➤ When you have described your problem situation and your so far unsuccessful coping strategy, pass your worksheet to the front.

   ☞ *If the group is small, have people place their worksheets face down in the center of the group.*

2. When all worksheets have been collected, announce that since other people don't have the same mindset or perspective, it's likely that they will see other options for coping with our situations.

3. Ask a volunteer to shuffle the worksheets and pass them around the group so that everyone gets someone else's worksheet. Give instructions for using them to pool the wisdom of other group members.

➤ As soon as you receive someone else's worksheet, read their problem and the strategy they've used for coping.

   ➤ Consider other possible strategies that might be useful in that situation.

   ➤ Write your suggested alternative in the first box for **Other strategies.**

   ➤ After you have added a new strategy to the first person's worksheet, pass it to the person on your left and collect a second person's worksheet from the person on your right.

➤ Read the problem and the strategies already suggested.

   ➤ Next, write your advice in the second box for **Other strategies.**

   ➤ Challenge yourself to come up with a practical approach that really fits the specific situation.

➤ Continue to shuffle papers and offer your most creative strategies for coping, until the worksheets are full of alternatives.

© 1997 Whole Person Associates 210 W Michigan Duluth MN 55802-1908   800-247-6789

➤ Work quickly and keep the process moving along.

➤ You will have 5 minutes total to think and write.

4. Supply everyone with masking tape. Ask them to hang all the worksheets on a blackboard or wall. Invite participants to find their own worksheet and silently read all the suggestions of other participants.

5. Ask for examples of helpful strategies generated by this process, congratulating volunteers for claiming their issues and proclaiming new coping options.

6. Encourage participants to leave their strategy sheets posted until the end of the session so others may read them during break times and benefit from the collective wisdom of the group.

Variations

▪ Focus on the specific problems of your audience (e.g., parenting dilemmas, work problems, relationship problems, communication issues, health concerns, family issues, spiritual dilemmas, group conflicts, addictive behaviors).

STRATEGY SHUFFLE

My situation

My strategy

Other strategies:

50 Personal Affirmation

In this powerful exercise, participants practice making self-affirmations and experiment with turning up the volume of positive self-talk.

Goals

To practice changing negative thoughts into positive, affirming ones.

To promote acceptance of new, positive beliefs about self.

Group size

Unlimited.

Time

15–20 minutes.

Materials

Blank paper; **Affirmations** worksheets; horn or harmonica; 4 posters (A: Shouting Station; B: Speaking Station; C: Whispering Station; D: Mouthing the Words Station).

Process

☞ *Before the session, hang the posters on one wall of the room. Spread them out about eight feet apart. A should be at the left and* **D** *at the right. In a small room, put one poster on each wall.*

1. Introduce the exercise with a few comments about the natural human need for affirmation and the paradox that we usually look outward rather than inward for this kind of positive judgment.

2. Distribute blank paper and ask participants to generate a personal affirmation list. (2–3 minutes)

➤ Make a list of ten statements you believe or would like to believe about yourself—affirmations such as *I am lovable; I am a competent person; I can achieve my goals; I'm a survivor; I can do anything I set my mind to*; or whatever positive statements you'd like to be able to make about yourself.

3. Hand out **Affirmations** worksheets and guide participants through the process of actively owning their affirmations. (10 minutes)

➤ On the wall are four stations, labeled A, B, C, and D. These represent different levels at which you might be willing to acknowledge the various affirmations you have written.

➤ Station A represents affirmations that you totally accept and would *shout* to the world.

➤ Station B represents statements you might *speak* aloud because you accept them sometimes.

➤ Station C represents affirmations that you are less sure of—ones which you might *whisper* or keep to yourself.

➤ Station D represents affirmations you do not really accept yet and would only *mouth the words* for.

➤ Stand up and go to the station that represents the extent to which you accept the first affirmation on your list.

➤ When you arrive at the station that best describes your acceptance of this affirmation, write the affirmation in the appropriate box—A, B, C, or D on your worksheet.

➤ Read the next affirmation on your list. Go to the station that best describes your acceptance of this affirmation and write it down in the appropriate box on your worksheet.

➤ Continue to work through your affirmations, one by one, traveling to the corresponding stations in order, until all ten affirmations have been put into one of the categories on your worksheet.

4. When most people have visited three or four stations, blow a

horn or harmonica to get the attention of participants and give instructions for practicing affirmations.

> Pair up with a neighbor at your present station and choose one of your affirmations you wish you believed more fully.

> Experiment by affirming this positive statement with more intensity. For example, if you can only whisper the words *It is okay to be human and make mistakes,* whisper them to your partner first, but then practice speaking these same words out loud to your partner. If you can speak the words but not shout them, try shouting them to your partner. Both of you practice several times. Then go back to your sorting and writing.

☞ *Give a brief role-play demonstration of how this works.*

5. After 1–2 minutes, blow the horn or harmonica again and ask participants to pair up with a new neighbor to practice turning up the volume on a different affirmation. Allow 3 minutes for practice, then instruct folks to continue sorting affirmations on their list according to the continuum.

☞ *Depending on time available and the energy level of the group, repeat Step 4 one or two more times.*

6. Ask everyone to return to their seats. Solicit examples of what participants learned about themselves during the affirmation practice. Summarize insights of the group, relating them to other issues or topics relevant to the group. (2–3 minutes).

Variations

▦ This is an excellent exercise for groups working on assertive behavior. Have people work along the continuum in teams of 3–4 people. During practice exercises, teams give short, specific positive suggestions for changes each person could make to enhance affirmations at higher levels. Acknowledge the improvements noticed in each practice episode.

AFFIRMATIONS

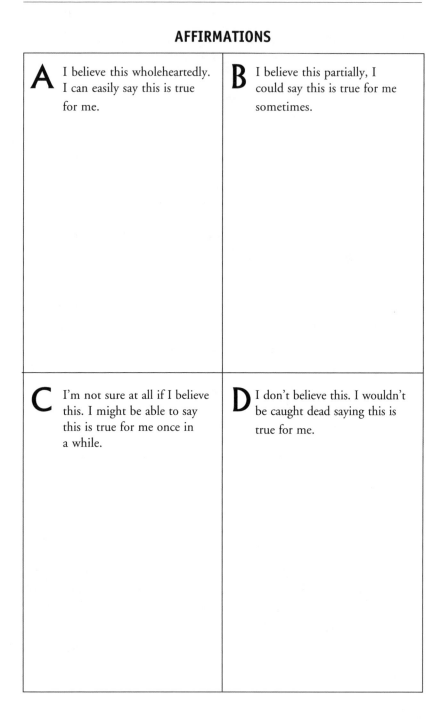

A I believe this wholeheartedly. I can easily say this is true for me.

B I believe this partially, I could say this is true for me sometimes.

C I'm not sure at all if I believe this. I might be able to say this is true for me once in a while.

D I don't believe this. I wouldn't be caught dead saying this is true for me.

Bibliography

Babior, Shirley, and Carol Goldman. *Working with Groups to Overcome Panic, Anxiety, & Phobias.* Duluth, Minn.: Whole Person Associates Inc., 1996.

Bailey, Roy. *50 Activities for Managing Stress.* Amherst, Mass.: HRD Press, 1989.

Belknap, Martha. *Mind-Body Magic: Creative Activities for Any Audience.* Duluth, Minn.: Whole Person Associates Inc., 1996.

Chang, Richard Y. *Creating High-Impact Training.* Irvine, Calif.: Richard Chang Associates Inc., 1994.

Christian, Sandy Stewart. *Working with Groups on Family Issues.* Duluth, Minn.: Whole Person Associates Inc., 1996.

———. *Working with Groups to Explore Food & Body Connections.* Duluth, Minn.: Whole Person Associates Inc., 1996.

Clark, Carolyn Chambers. *Creating a Climate for Power Learning: 37 Mind-Stretching Activities.* Duluth, Minn.: Whole Person Associates Inc., 1997.

Czimbal, Bob, and Maggie Zadikov. *Stress Survival Kit.* Portland, Ore.: Open Book Publishers, 1992.

———. *Vitamin T: A Guide to Healthy Touch.* Portland, Ore.: Open Book Publishers, 1991.

Dossick, Jane, and Eugene Shea. *Creative Therapy II: 52 More Exercises for Groups.* Sarasota, Fla.: Professional Resources Exchange Inc., 1990.

———. *Creative Therapy: 52 Exercises for Groups.* Sarasota, Fla: Professional Resources Exchange Inc., 1988.

Eberhardt, Louise Yolton. *Working with Groups in the Workplace: Bridging the Gender Gap.* Duluth, Minn.: Whole Person Associates Inc., 1995.

———. *Working with Groups in the Workplace:* Confronting Sexual Harassment. Duluth, Minn.: Whole Person Associates Inc., 1995.

———. *Working with Women's Groups, Volumes 1 & 2.* Duluth, Minn.: Whole Person Associates Inc., 1994.

Eitington, Julius E. *The Winning Trainer.* Houston: Gulf Publishing Company, 1989.

Fluegelman, Andrew, ed. *The New Games Book.* San Francisco, Calif.: The Headlands Press, 1976.

Forbess-Green, Sue. *The Encyclopedia of Icebreakers: Structured Activities that Warm-Up, Motivate, Challenge, Acquaint, and Energize.* San Diego, Calif.: Applied Skill Press, 1980.

Hart, Lois B., *50 Activities for Developing Leaders.* Amherst, Mass.: HRD Press, 1994.

Hart, Lois B., *Connections: 125 Activities for Faultless Training.* Amherst, Mass.: HRD Press, 1995.

Hetherington, Cheryl. *Working with Groups from Dysfunctional Families.* Duluth, Minn.: Whole Person Associates Inc., 1994.

———. *Working with Groups in the Workplace: Celebrating Diversity.* Duluth, Minn.: Whole Person Associates Inc., 1995.

Higgins, James M. *101 Creative Problem Solving Techniques.* Winter Park, Fla: The New Management Publishing Company, 1994.

Hopkins, Elaine, et al. *Working with Groups on Spiritual Themes.* Duluth, Minn.: Whole Person Associates Inc., 1995.

Karsk, Roger, and Bill Thomas. *Working with Men's Groups.* Duluth, Minn.: Whole Person Associates Inc., 1995.

Kreitlow, Burton, and Doris Kreitlow. *Creative Planning for the Second Half of Life.* Duluth, Minn.: Whole Person Associates Inc, 1996.

Lazear, David. *Seven Ways of Teaching.* Palatine, Ill.: IRI/Skylight Publishing Inc., 1991.

Lusk, Julie T. *30 Scripts for Relaxation, Imagery, & Inner Healing, Volumes 1 & 2.* Duluth, Minn.: Whole Person Associates Inc., 1993.

Nason, Cheryl. *How to Convince People You Know What You're Talking About: A Guide to Improving Presentation Skills.* Arlington, Tex.: Nason/Harris Associates, 1995.

Newstrom, John W. *Still More Games Trainers Play.* New York: McGraw Hill, 1991.

Newstrom, John W., and Edward E. Scannell. *Games Trainers Play.* New York: McGraw-Hill, 1980.

Nilson, Carolyn. *Team Games for Trainers.* New York: McGraw-Hill, 1993.

Peoples, David A. *Presentations Plus.* New York: John Wiley & Sons, 1992.

Queen, Sandy. *Wellness Activities for Youth, Volumes 1 & 2.* Duluth, Minn.: Whole Person Associates Inc., 1994.

Rohnke, Karl. *Silver Bullets: A Guide to Initiative Problems, Adventure Games, and Trust Activities.* Dubuque, Iowa: Kendall/Hunt Publishing Company, 1984.

Scannell, Edward E., and John W. Newstrom. *More Games Trainers Play.* New York: McGraw-Hill, 1983.

Scearce, Carol. *100 Ways to Build Teams.* Palatine, Ill.: IRI/Skylight Publishing, 1992.

Schwartz, Andrew E. *Guided Imagery for Groups.* Duluth, Minn.: Whole Person Associates Inc., 1995.

Senge, Peter M., Art Kleiner, and Charlotte Roberts. *The Fifth Discipline Fieldbook: Strategies for Building a Learning Organization.* New York: Doubleday, 1994.

Stern, Nancy, and Maggi Payment. *101 Stupid Things Trainers Do to Sabotage Success.* Irvine, Calif.: Richard Chang Associates Inc., 1995.

Tubesing, Nancy Loving, Donald A. Tubesing, and Sandy Stewart Christian, eds. *Structured Exercises in Stress Management, Volumes 1–5.* Duluth, Minn.: Whole Person Associates Inc., 1994–1996.

Tubesing, Nancy Loving, Donald A. Tubesing, and Sandy Stewart Christian, eds. *Structured Exercises in Wellness Promotion, Volumes 1–5.* Duluth, Minn.: Whole Person Associates Inc., 1994–1996.

Wade, Pamela A. *Producing High-Impact Learning Tools.* Irvine, Calif.: Richard Chang Associates Inc., 1995.

Weinstein, Matt, and Joel Goodman. *Playfair.* San Luis Obispo, Calif.: Impact Publishers, 1980.

Williamson, Bruce. *Playful Activities for Powerful Presentations.* Duluth, Minn.: Whole Person Associates Inc., 1993.

DISCOVER MORE PLAYFUL ICEBREAKERS
in these companion resources from Whole Person Associates

PLAYFUL ACTIVITIES FOR POWERFUL PRESENTATIONS
Bruce Williamson

Spice up presentations with healthy laughter. The 40 creative energizers in *Playful Activities for Powerful Presentations* will enhance learning, stimulate communication, promote teamwork, and reduce resistance to group interaction.

❏ Playful Activities for Powerful Presentations / $21.95

MIND-BODY MAGIC
Creative Activities for Any Audience
Martha Belknap, MA

Make any presentation more powerful with one of these 40 feel-good activities. Handy tips with each activity show you how to use it in your presentation, plus ideas for enhancing or extending the activity, and suggestions for adapting it for your teaching goals and audience. Use *Mind-Body Magic* to present any topic with pizzazz!

❏ Mind-Body Magic / $21.95
❏ Worksheet Masters / $9.95

PLAYING ALONG
37 Group Learning Activities Borrowed from Improvisational Theater
Izzy Gesell, MS

Novice-friendly improvisational theater techniques adapted for community or workplace groups focused on personal development or organizational change. Use these intriguing tools in presentations, workshops, or classes to build self-esteem, encourage creative thinking, promote team building, and support problem solving.

❏ Playing Along / $21.95

CREATING A CLIMATE FOR POWER LEARNING
37 Mind-Stretching Activities
Carolyn Chambers Clark, EdD, ARNP

Creative warmup processes that prepare leaders and participants for a satisfying learning experience. These activities will enhance your presentation skills, leadership style, and teaching effectiveness no matter what your audience or setting.

❏ Creating a Climate for Power Learning / $21.95

ACTIVITY-IN-A-BAG: FORTUNE COOKIES
Emphasize key concepts, provide an upbeat closing for your session, and move participants to embrace desired goals and changes with this light-hearted but effective learning-reinforcement activity. Fifty colorful latex balloons plus a "fortune" message pad turn affirmation and goal-setting exercises into an energetic, interactive process.

❏ Fortune Cookies / $15.95

© 1997 Whole Person Associates 210 W Michigan Duluth MN 55802-1908   800-247-6789

FIND CREATIVE TOPICAL ICEBREAKERS
in these structured learning exercises
volumes from Whole Person Associates

Working with Groups to EXPLORE FOOD & BODY CONNECTIONS
Sandy Stewart Christian, MSW, editor

This innovative collection of 36 group processes tackles complex and painful issues nearly everyone is concerned about—dieting, weight, healthy eating, fitness, body image, and self-esteem—using a whole person approach that advocates health and fitness for people of all sizes.

❑ Working with Groups to Explore Food & Body Connections / $24.95
❑ Worksheet Masters / $9.95

Working with Groups on FAMILY ISSUES
Sandy Stewart Christian, MSW, LICSW, editor

These 24 structured exercises combine the knowledge of marriage and family experts with practical techniques to help you move individuals, couples, and families toward positive change.

❑ Working with Groups on Family Issues / $24.95
❑ Worksheet Masters / $9.95

Working with Groups from DYSFUNCTIONAL FAMILIES
Cheryl Hetherington

This collection of 29 proven group activities is designed to heal the pain that results from living in a dysfunctional family. With these exercises leaders can promote healing, build self-esteem, encourage sharing, and help participants acknowledge their feelings.

❑ Working with Groups from Dysfunctional Families / $24.95
❑ Worksheet Masters / $9.95

Working with Groups on SPIRITUAL THEMES
Elaine Hopkins, Zo Woods, Russell Kelley, Katrina Bentley, and James Murphy

The material contained in this manual helps health professionals initiate discussion on spiritual needs in a logical, organized fashion that induces a high level of comfort for group members and leaders.

❑ Working with Groups on Spiritual Themes / $24.95
❑ Worksheet Masters / $9.95

Working with Groups in the Workplace: CELEBRATING DIVERSITY
Cheryl Hetherington

Celebrating Diversity helps people confront and question the beliefs, prejudices, and fears that can separate them from others. Carefully written exercises help trainers present these sensitive issues in the workplace as well as in educational settings.

❑ Celebrating Diversity / $24.95
❑ Worksheet Masters / $9.95

© 1997 Whole Person Associates 210 W Michigan Duluth MN 55802-1908   800-247-6789

STOCK UP ON STRESS MANAGEMENT AND HEALTH-ORIENTED ICEBREAKERS
from the stress and wellness specialists at
Whole Person Associates

Structured Exercises in STRESS MANAGEMENT, Volumes 1–5
Structured Exercises in WELLNESS PROMOTION, Volumes 1–5
Nancy Loving Tubesing, EdD, Donald A. Tubesing, PhD,
and Sandy Stewart Christian, MSW, editors

Developed by an interdisciplinary team of leaders in the wellness movement nation-
wide and top stress management professionals, these exercises actively encourage
participants to examine their current attitudes and patterns. All process designs are
clearly explained and have been thoroughly field-tested with diverse
audiences so that trainers can use them with confidence.

Each volume brims with practical ideas that mix and match,
allowing trainers to develop new programs for varied settings,
audiences, and time frames. Each volume contains **Icebreakers,
Action Planners, Closing Processes,** and **Group Energizers.** The
Wellness Promotion volumes also include **Wellness Explorations** and
Self-Care Strategies. The *Stress Management* volumes include **Stress
Assessments, Management Strategies,** and **Skill Builders.**

- ❑ Stress or Wellness 8 1/2" x 11" Loose-leaf Edition—
   Vols 1–5 / $54.95 each
- ❑ Stress or Wellness 6" x 9" Softcover Edition—Vols 1–5 / $29.95 each
- ❑ Worksheet Masters—Vols 1–5 / $9.95 each
   ** Worksheet Masters are included as part of the loose-leaf edition.**

WELLNESS ACTIVITIES FOR YOUTH, Volumes 1 & 2
Sandy Queen

Each volume of *Wellness Activities for Youth* provides 36 complete classroom activities
that help leaders teach children and teenagers about wellness with a whole person approach and an emphasis on FUN. The concepts include: values, stress and coping, self-
esteem, personal well-being, and social wellness.

- ❑ Wellness Activities for Youth, Vols 1 & 2 / $21.95 each
- ❑ Worksheet Masters / $9.95 each

ACTIVITY-IN-A-BAG: PILEUP CARD GAME
This fun and unique card game contains 108 colorful stress and
coping cards, a spinner, and an easy-to-follow activity book for
eight different games that can be used with all age groups to make
learning about stress management fun. An extra deck of cards is
recommended for groups of ten or more.

- ❑ PileUp Card Games / $15.95
- ❑ Cards only / $7.95

EXPLORE GENDER-RELATED ISSUES WITH ICEBREAKERS
from Whole Person Associates' *Working with Groups* resources

WORKING WITH WOMEN'S GROUPS, Volumes 1 & 2
Louise Yolton Eberhardt

Volume 1 explores consciousness raising, self-discovery, and assertiveness training. *Volume 2* looks at sexuality issues, women of color, and leadership skills training.

❏ Working with Women's Groups, Vols 1 & 2 / $24.95 each
❏ Worksheet Masters Vols 1 & 2 / $9.95 each

WORKING WITH MEN'S GROUPS
Roger Karsk and Bill Thomas

Working with Men's Groups has been updated to reflect the reality of men's lives in the 1990s. Each exercise helps trainers develop either onetime workshops or ongoing groups that explore men's issues in four key areas: self-discovery, consciousness raising, intimacy, and parenting.

❏ Working with Men's Groups / $24.95
❏ Worksheet Masters / $9.95

Working with Groups in the Workplace:
BRIDGING THE GENDER GAP
Louise Yolton Eberhardt

Bridging the Gender Gap contains a wealth of exercises for trainers to use with men and women who work as colleagues. These activities will also be useful in gender role awareness groups, diversity training, couples workshops, college classes, and youth seminars.

❏ Bridging the Gender Gap / $24.95
❏ Worksheet Masters / $9.95

Working with Groups in the Workplace:
CONFRONTING SEXUAL HARRASSMENT
Louise Yolton Eberhardt

Confronting Sexual Harassment presents exercises that trainers can safely use with groups to constructively explore the issues of sexual harassment, look at the underlying causes, understand the law, motivate men to become allies, and empower women to speak up.

❏ Confronting Sexual Harassment / $24.95
❏ Worksheet Masters / $9.95

ACTIVITY-IN-A-BAG: WOMEN IN ART POSTCARD SERIES
Move participants toward new ways of thinking by helping them discover their own beauty, creativity, and uniqueness in this unusual set of kits. Each kit includes 25 fine art postcards and complete instructions for using those cards in your session.

❏ Kit 1: Image & Self-Image. Explore issues of self-esteem. / $24.95
❏ Kit 2: Beauty & the Beholder. Investigates gender issues related to cultural stereotypes and images of beauty. / $24.95
❏ Kit 3: Romanticism & Realism. Examines family and other significant relationships. / $24.95
❏ Kit 4: Multicultural Gallery. Affirms personal heritage and explores its impact on individuals. / $24.95

© 1997 Whole Person Associates 210 W Michigan Duluth MN 55802-1908   800-247-6789

Whole Person Products

STRESS AND WELLNESS SERIES
* Structured Exercises in Stress Management, Volumes 1–5 (softcover) .. each $29.95
Structured Exercises in Stress Management, Volumes 1–5 (loose-leaf).. each $54.95
* Structured Exercises in Wellness Promotion, Volumes 1–5 (softcover) . each $29.95
Structured Exercises in Wellness Promotion, Volumes 1–5 (loose-leaf). each $54.95
Stress & Wellness Reference Guide (index to series) $29.95

TOOLS FOR WORKING WITH GROUPS
* Working with Women's Groups, Volumes 1 & 2 .... each $24.95
* Working with Men's Groups $24.95
* Working with Groups from Dysfunctional Families $24.95
* Working with Groups on Spiritual Themes $24.95
* Celebrating Diversity $24.95
* Bridging the Gender Gap $24.95
* Confronting Sexual Harassment $24.95
* Working with Groups to Explore Food & Body Connections $24.95
* Working with Groups to Overcome Panic, Anxiety, & Phobias $24.95
* Working with Groups to Explore Family Issues $24.95
* Working with Groups: Creative Planning for the Second Half of Life $24.95
* Instant Icebreakers $24.95

WORKING WITH YOUNG PEOPLE
* Wellness Activities for Youth, Volumes 1 & 2 .... each $21.95
What Do You Do with a Child Like This? $15.95

*Companion Worksheet Masters are available for all books marked with a *
Worksheet Masters .... each volume $9.95

TRAINERS RESOURCES
Playful Activities for Powerful Presentations $21.95
Mind-Body Magic $21.95
Creating a Climate for Power Learning $21.95
Playing Along $21.95
30 Scripts for Relaxation, Imagery, & Inner Healing, Volumes 1 & 2 . each $21.95
Inquire Within (imagery/meditation) $21.95
Guided Imagery for Groups $24.95
Mind-Body Wellness: An Annotated Bibliography $29.95
TOOTS for Trainers $10.00

SELF-HELP BOOKS
Kicking Your Stress Habits $15.95
Seeking Your Healthy Balance $15.95
Overcoming Panic, Anxiety, & Phobias $12.95
Sleep Secrets $12.95
Don't Get Mad, Get Funny! $12.95

VIDEO COURSES
Making Healthy Choices Series (6 videos, Leader & Skill Building Guides) . $475.00
  Single session videos available (each tape includes 5 guides) .... each $95.00
    Session 1: Healthy Lifestyle / Session 2: Healthy Eating /
    Session 3: Healthy Exercise / Session 4: Healthy Stress /
    Session 5: Healthy Relationships / Session 6: Healthy Change

Managing Job Stress Series (6 videos, Leader & Skill Building Guides) $475.00
  Single session videos available (each tape includes 5 guides) .... each $95.00
    Session 1: Handling Workplace Pressure / Session 2: Clarifying Roles
    and Expectations / Session 3: Controlling the Workload / Session 4:
    Managing People Pressures / Session 5: Surviving the Changing
    Workplace / Session 6: Balancing Work and Home

© 1997 Whole Person Associates 210 W Michigan Duluth MN 55802-1908   800-247-6789

Manage It! Series (6 videos, Leader & Skill Building Guides) $475.00
Single session videos available (each tape includes 5 guides) .... each $95.00
   Session 1: Stress Traps / Session 2: Stress Overload / Session 3: Interper-
   sonal Conflict / Session 4: Addictive Patterns / Session 5: Job Stress /
   Session 6: Survival Skills

GROUP ACTIVITY KITS
PileUp $15.95
   extra cards $7.95
Activity in a Bag: Fortune Cookie $15.95
Women in Art Postcard Series
   Kit 1: Image & Self-Image $24.95
   Kit 2: Beauty & the Beholder $24.95
   Kit 3: Romanticism & Realism $24.95
   Kit 4: Multicultural Gallery $24.95

AUDIO RESOURCES (Relaxation, Meditation, and Guided Imagery)
Stress Breaks
   BreakTime $11.95
   Natural Tranquilizers $11.95
   Stress Escapes $11.95
   Worry Stoppers $11.95
Daydreams
   Daydreams 1: Getaways $11.95
   Daydreams 2: Peaceful Places $11.95
   Daydreams 3: Relaxing Retreats $11.95
Sensational Relaxation
   Countdown to Relaxation $11.95
   Daybreak / Sundown $11.95
   Take a Deep Breath $11.95
   Relax . . . Let Go . . . Relax $11.95
   Stress Release $11.95
   Warm & Heavy $11.95
Mini Meditations
   Healing Visions $11.95
   Refreshing Journeys $11.95
   Healthy Choices $11.95
Guided Meditation
   Inner Healing $11.95
   Personal Empowering $11.95
   Healthy Balancing $11.95
   Spiritual Centering $11.95
   Mantras $11.95
Do-It-Yourself Relaxation
   Yoga $11.95
   Massage $11.95
Do-It-Yourself Wellness
   Eating $11.95
   Body Image $11.95
   Calm Down $11.95
Relaxation/Meditation Music
   Tranquility $11.95
   Harmony $11.95
   Serenity $11.95
   Contemplation (CD) $15.95

About Whole Person Associates

At Whole Person Associates we're 100% committed to practical trainers tools and innovative self-help resources that actively involve participants and provide a "whole person" focus—body, mind, spirit, relationships, lifestyle.

ABOUT THE OWNERS

Whole Person Associates was created by the vision of two people: Donald A. Tubesing, PhD, and Nancy Loving Tubesing, EdD. Don and Nancy have been active in the stress management/wellness promotion movement for over twenty years—consulting, leading seminars, writing, and publishing. Most of our early products were the result of their creativity and expertise. Living proof that you can "stay evergreen," Don and Nancy remain the driving force behind the company and are still very active in developing new products that touch people's lives.

ABOUT THE COMPANY

Whole Person Associates was "born" in Duluth, Minnesota, and we remain committed to our lovely city on the shore of Lake Superior. We put the same high quality into every product we offer, translating the best of current research into practical, accessible, easy-to-use materials. We create the best possible resources to help our customers teach about stress management, whole person wellness promotion, and workplace productivity issues. And our friendly, resourceful employees are committed to helping you find the products that fit your needs.

We also strive to treat our customers as we would like to be treated. If we fall short of our goals in any way, please let us know.

ABOUT OUR ASSOCIATES

Who are the "associates" in Whole Person Associates? They're the trainers, therapists, health educators, group leaders, authors, musicians, and others who have shared their expertise in this book and other whole person resources featured here. All of our products were developed by experts who are leaders in their fields. We're very proud to be associated with them.

ABOUT OUR CUSTOMERS

We'd love to hear from you! Let us know what you think of our products— how you use them in your work, what additional materials you'd like to see us develop, and what shortcomings you've noted. Write us, call toll-free 800-247-6789, or visit our Web site at www.wholeperson.com. We look forward to hearing from you!

www.wholeperson.com

Call 1-800-247-6789 to receive a catalog or to place an order.